THE ACCOMMODATION

THE
Accommodation

The Politics of Race in an American City

JIM SCHUTZE

CITADEL PRESS
SECAUCUS, NEW JERSEY

Published by Citadel Press
A division of Lyle Stuart Inc.
120 Enterprise Avenue, Secaucus, N.J. 07094
In Canada: Musson Book Company
A division of General Publishing Co. Limited
Don Mills, Ontario

Library of Congress Cataloging-in-Publication Data

Schutze, Jim.
    The accommodation.

    1. Dallas (Tex.) — Race relations. 2. Afro-Americans —
Texas — Dallas — Politics and government. 3. Afro-
Americans — Civil rights — Texas — Dallas. I. Title.
F394.D219N47   1986   305.8'0097642812   86-1946
ISBN 0-8065-1046-3

Printed in the United States of America

For Mariana and for Dallas,
my happy discoveries.

THE ACCOMMODATION

1

Reporters covering the secret proceedings of the grand jury watched for minuscule clues to what was going on inside the jury's locked chamber, hanging on every change of expression or posture as the jurors appeared in the courthouse corridors and then disappeared again into their sanctum. They watched to see which witnesses were called and what their mood was, hoping for the occasional scrap thrown them by an insider. They hovered and worked the corridor outside the chamber. It was hot in September of 1951, and the air-conditioning was still running in the old red sandstone courthouse at the river end of downtown Dallas.

Henry Wade, the new young Dallas County district attorney, spent an hour with the grand jurors inside their air-conditioned room. Wade was brand-new in office and untested. In the next decade, when a deranged drifter would gun down the President of the United States in Dallas, Wade would appear in the national press as the tough, shrewd, bull-shouldered, tobacco-chewing district attorney who saw to it that Jack Ruby, the murderer's murderer, wouldn't slip through the bonds of the law on a shrink plea.

By the 1960s, and even before the assassination, Wade was well on his way to the status of local legend, third-generation successor to a proud Texas family tradition. His father had been a judge and his grandfather had sponsored the Wade Amendment, making the guarantee of free public education a part of the 1876 state constitution adopted at the end of Reconstruction. As an assistant district attorney in the late 1940s, Wade had worked with black leaders in Dallas to bring the black community within the bounds and under the protection of the system of law, which, for Wade, meant fighting for penitentiary convictions of black people who murdered other black people. Until then, one black's murder of another had been treated by all-white juries in Dallas as a sort of misdemeanor, almost always punished with a short suspended sentence.

But in 1951, Henry Wade was still a question mark. He had been elected district attorney in November 1950, had taken office the following January, and his first concern was this enormously delicate, controversial, literally explosive grand jury investigation. He was a young man, making his way.

When Wade left the air-conditioned deliberation room, the reporters who were staking out the grand jury in the corridor looked him over closely and noticed that he was sweating. They could see an anteroom on the other side of the window in the locked hallway door. At one point, some of the jurors came out into the anteroom and argued with each other, silent through the glass but clearly bickering. They disappeared back into the room at the back. Then, at 6 p.m., bailiff Bert Whisnand hurried out of the room and down the echoing corridor to the chambers of Judge Henry King. The proceedings of the grand jury were shrouded in thick secrecy, but during Whisnand's brief progress from the grand jury room to the judge's chambers, it became unofficially known to the hubbub of reporters who had been waiting in the corridor all day that the august body behind the closed doors was not going to issue the report it had promised for that day. Certain things might happen the next day, on Saturday. Shoulders were shrugged, and doors were closed.

There was nothing for anyone to do about that. The chances of anyone writing a sharply aimed story about possible division and rancor on the grand jury were negligible. The news media in Dallas did not produce sharply aimed stories about anything at that point in their history. Television was not yet even a voice in the Vulgate of local news. The two newspapers, The Dallas Morning News and the Dallas Times Herald, had carved up the market comfortably between them, the Morning News taking the conservative, monied side of the tracks, and the Herald speaking mainly to the working classes, but both were still locally owned and were complete and obedient creatures of the sternly controlled political culture of the city. Because the Herald didn't have to curry favor with the city's extremely conservative upper-middle class, it sometimes kicked up a little more dust than the Morning News, but neither newspaper was going to kick up anything at all in this case.

If any news medium, cleric, labor organizer, or sidewalk prophet had raised Cain about anything in Dallas in 1951, it would not have been about this particular grand jury, even though everyone in the corridor that day knew very well something strange was going on. The jurors were battling. Something had gone wrong. Whatever went wrong with this particular grand jury would have deep repercussions in the city. This was not, after all, an ordinary grand jury. This was the "blue ribbon" grand jury, and the crimes it was investigating were crimes close to the very soul of the city.

The reporters in the corridor, like the rest of the community, assumed these men could find out whatever they wanted to find and say whatever they wanted to say. And only a month before, the grand jury had seemed to promise startling results. In a prepared statement and speaking as a body, the jurors had announced, "All law enforcement agencies have cooperated to the fullest to dig out every angle and are continuing to do so. We will pursue every angle from the planning of these crimes to the actual throwing of a bomb or burning of a house. Our community must not suffer from the impulsive acts of a few. Peace and tolerance in every section of Dallas is our aim, and it will be accomplished by the elimination of lawlessness. We ask for understanding and tolerance from all citizens of Dallas, and the matter will be satisfactorily concluded."

Now, after a year of suspense, of surprise witnesses and indictments, the clock had struck and the hour had come for an answer to the riddle, for the name of the mastermind and the name of his punishment.

But something had happened in the grand jury room that day. The reporters could see it in the shadows, smell it in the dust, feel it in the expressions of the jurors who mouthed silently and angrily on the other side of a windowed door. They could see it written in the sweat on Henry Wade's face. Perhaps, even then, even on that day, everyone — everyone in Dallas who knew anything or anybody — felt somewhere in his or her bones what the answer would be. By then it was all over town, almost as soon as it was convened, that the grand jury had found itself dredging up dirty fistfuls of things it had never wanted to see, connections between these unspeakable crimes and respectable middle-class neighborhood groups, even church groups.

3

The bombings, in other words, might have come right up out of the spiritual heart of the white community, the heart darkened by 19th-century spectres.

2

In 1950, for the second time in a decade, the City of Dallas was in serious danger of racial warfare. The dynamitings of black middle-class homes had started again. None of the measures adopted after a wave of bombings 10 years earlier had had lasting effect. The tendency of the city for organized and violent white aggression against blacks seemed ineluctable. It was the chain that tied the city to a bloody past.

Even more than the rest of East and North Texas, Dallas had been plagued with outbreaks of violence and Ku Klux Klan activity off and on since Reconstruction. At times, in the first part of the century, Dallas seemed to be the epicenter of Klan violence in the country, certainly in the Southwest. Dallas commands a part of Texas that is much more Southern, with stronger roots in slave culture, than many outsiders realize. But for all the penchant the city seemed to show for sheets and lynching, the commercial ruling class of Dallas had already, in the early 20th century, begun to show a strong inclination for control and pacification.

In the late 1920s, a number of leading families and the business community, led by The Dallas Morning News, had driven racial terror back beneath the surface of the city. The Morning News had taken the lead in an anti-Klan campaign that had come at the right moment and had proved enormously effective, almost as if the Klan's own adherents were happy to have an excuse to get out. Yet there was always a sense that violent racism still lived somewhere, enlivened by bombings of black families in the early 1940s and now, again, by another wave of dynamite attacks in the early 1950s. A special investigation in 1955 by the Texas Attorney General would find strong evidence of a Klan resurgence in East Texas. While the Klan was never mentioned publicly in connection with the Dallas bombings of the early 1950s, the attacks did seem, the more they were investigated, to have strong organized roots, even religious roots, in the middle-class and blue-collar white community — a pattern that was all too familiar to those who had lived through earlier terrors.

The true leadership of the city, which had been honing its oligarchical style since the 1930s, had never condoned bombing and lynching. And the bombings in the early 1950s could not have come at a worse moment. The oligarchy of land developers who were just then consolidating their control over Dallas had lavish dreams for the future that could be spoiled by racial war. The Sunbelt phenomenon, now one of the major facts of the nation's history in this century, was already a gleam in the eyes of a few wild schemers in 1950, men who would have been ridiculed for their ideas had they discussed them openly. If their dreams were outlandish, they were also ferocious, and the developers were damned if they were going to allow the familiar presence of racial terror to spoil everything. And so they had waded in themselves, these business princes of the city. They had named either themselves or their seconds to this special grand jury, called to find out who was behind the wave of dynamite bombings and arson attacks sweeping South Dallas.

South Dallas, now almost entirely black, was then, only a quarter century ago, almost entirely white. The wealthy Jews who had lived along South Boulevard had departed, and the middle-class Jewish and Christian communities were already beginning to pack up and trek north, family by family, but the massive transposition of whites from South to North Dallas was still a few years off. In 1950 and 1951, South Dallas was still the best home many of its white residents had ever known. It was also the embattled border country between the racial tribes, the unsettled terrain where the white tribe and the black tribe fought for territory and where the rituals of racial tribalism devolved into violence.

Even before World War II, before numbers of blacks had the ability to buy and live in good houses, the Southern half of the city had been the battleground where blacks had sought to expand their reach. A wave of dynamitings of black homes had frightened the city's business

6

leaders in the early 1940s and had inspired the creation of an evolving series of "racial committees" to promote dialogue between leaders in the black and white communities. But the racial committees had not turned the trick. Now the bombings had returned with an awful fury, and it was clear that only strong new measures could stop them.

The stature of the men who sat on the special grand jury was a dramatic demonstration that Dallas' white business leaders knew no matter what they had done before, they had not done enough. The grand jurors were not just prominent men. They were the Who's Who of the city — Ray Hubbard, oilman and park board president; James Ralph Wood, president of Southwestern Life Insurance Company and an organizer of the Dallas Crime Commission; Bernard F. McLain, president of Hart Furniture Company and a civic booster; William H. Cothrum Sr., who built medium-rent apartments and homes for both black and white tenants; Julius Schepps, a wholesale liquor distributor, civic booster and leader in the Jewish community; Jacob Golman, president of the Oak Cliff Baking Company; Clarence A. Tatum Jr., vice president of Dallas Power and Light Company; William J. Durham, a black attorney; the Reverend Bezaleel R. Riley, a black minister; James F. Chambers Jr., managing editor of the Dallas Times Herald; James C. Dycus, president of the Oak Cliff Bank and Trust Company; P.B. (Jack) Garrett, president of the Texas Bank and Trust Company; John T. Higginbotham, president of Higginbotham-Bailey Company; and the Reverend Robert Lawrence Parish, a black minister.

The special majesty implied in the jury's designation as a "blue ribbon" body required a small amount of hocus pocus, in order to bend the customs of Anglo-Saxon law around to the reality of Dallas politics. Today, sitting behind his desk on the top floor of the Dallas County Courthouse, speaking from the summit of a long and legendary career, a white-maned Henry Wade can say, "Of course there's no such thing as a blue-ribbon grand jury. You appoint not less than three nor more than five grand jury commissioners, and they pick not less than 16 nor more than 20 jurors, and that's a grand jury."

But the grand jury commissioners appointed in this case were all members of the Dallas Citizens Council, as were almost all of the jurors they subpoenaed to serve, the white ones, anyway. Their combined personal might and power in the community was clearly intended to send a political message that was at least as important as the technical law-enforcement role of the grand jury as a gatherer of evidence and bringer of indictments.

Jim Chambers, called back from a vacation in Wisconsin to serve, sits behind his own desk today at Scottish Rite Hospital in the Oak Lawn section of Dallas, where he serves as the hospital's unpaid but punctiliously present chairman of the board. Chambers remembers, too, that the grand jurors set out on their mission with political and social goals in mind at least as prominently as the strictly legal task of bringing the bombers to justice. When he talks about the grand jury, Chambers often uses the phrase, "Dallas as a whole," which was the emblematic phrasing the Citizens Council always used in its heyday to signal its own authority, wisdom, and concern for the greater good of the city.

"The Citizens Council was groping for a message to the black community, that Dallas as a whole didn't tolerate what was going on in this South Dallas community. To give lip service just wasn't enough. It was a two-pronged situation, to let the blacks know we didn't subscribe to this, and to stop the thing."

The names of the jurors alone should have struck fear in the heart of anyone who ever hoped to do business in Dallas. But, as it developed, the people the grand jury questioned were not always susceptible to those pressures, either because they knew they were innocent or because they didn't believe the grand jury could do much to them if they weren't.

When Charles O. Goff was hauled in, he and his pals were sneering in their contempt for Wade, for the blue-ribbon grand jury, for the lot of them. Goff, a business agent for the lathers' union, was a prominent figure in South Dallas politics. He had helped organize a slate for the city council in 1947 in an unsuccessful bid to wrest control of City Hall away from the business titans. He was an active defender of the interests of his neighborhood in Exline Park, an area of small, new, frame homes built for working- and middle-class people after the war. Goff was chairman of the Exline Park Improvement League, one of many "improvement leagues," citizens councils and groups of other descriptions and titles dotting the white neighborhoods of the city by then, all organized with a strong emphasis on race. Goff, who had appeared often before the Dallas City Council to discuss black housing issues, was known to the larger community. He was no nameless thug.

He was charged as an accomplice in the bombing of Leo's Grocery and Market at 4208 Oakland. No sooner had he been brought in, smiling beneath a shock of gray hair, than two of his neighbors, Maury

Hughes and Louis Reinle, showed up to post his bond. The pair told reporters they were "friends and neighbors" of Goff, not professional bondsmen. Hughes, a lawyer, joked with the reporters that Goff's trial should be held in City Park, since no courtroom would be big enough to hold his supporters.

Their cocksure defiance and the suggestion that they had the political sympathy of the city's white working and middle class behind them presented an ugly prospect indeed for the oligarchy. Everything the leadership had been able to do during the forties to damp the recurring flames of racial tension seemed, instead, to have wound up fanning the fire. All of the temporary solutions had only worsened the fundamental problems — a vicious housing shortage for blacks.

After the bombings of the 1940s, the city had gone in under some color of the law, now very obscure, and had bought away the homes of black people who had made the mistake of buying property in white neighborhoods. The homes were then rented by the city or sold to white owners, this time encumbered with deed restrictions thick with all sorts of South African formulas for racial composition and distribution, requiring the new owners not to sell to blacks for 50 years or until the block on which their home stood had become at least 50 percent black-owned. In 1944, the city announced proudly that it had turned a tidy profit on several of the properties it had taken from blacks and resold to whites.

By the late 1940s, the black slums of Dallas were so hideous that they were arousing the consciences of white leaders like Mayor Wallace Savage and a courageous young retailing executive named Joseph Roos among others. The white business oligarchy was beginning to admit to itself by then that the black slums of West Dallas, Mill Creek, and elsewhere in scattered sites on the periphery of the city — all throwbacks to Reconstruction, unsoftened by the 20th century — were no longer conscionable and, not incidentally, were no longer good for business.

The slums in the area along the Trinity River called West Dallas contained less than 20 percent of Dallas County's population outside Dallas proper but accounted for 50 percent of the typhus, 60 percent of the tuberculosis and 30 percent of the polio in the unincorporated portion of the county. Infant death rates were unmeasured but were generally believed to be staggering. No water or sewer lines ran to the slums. Water was sold from barrels, and people urinated and

9

defecated into holes in the ground. Depressions where gravel had been scoured away for use in construction were filled with water and stood stagnant and swarming with mosquitoes and flies. Families huddled in shacks and sheds made of packing crates and junk.

A cruel vice-grip dynamic was operating on the population levels of the black slums: black population citywide was growing at only a modest rate, much less than the rate of white growth, so that the overall ratio of black to white in Dallas had dropped from 17.1 percent in 1940 to 13.1 percent in 1950. But, as the white community consolidated itself in new areas and forced the scattered ragtag bands of black settlers out of their environs, the population levels of the few slums where blacks were still welcome, often the meanest, were becoming enormously more dense. Eagle Ford in West Dallas, where property was advertised in the newspaper under the heading, "Colored Lots," grew by 1500 percent during the decade of the forties.

Much of the slum property in Dallas was owned by white absentees. Joseph Roos, a director of the Dallas Council of Social Agencies, pasted back the ears of the members of the Dallas Junior Chamber of Commerce in 1951 when he told their assemblage at the Adolphus Hotel that 100,000 human beings in Dallas were living in 36,560 shacks, of which 61.4 percent were rented from landlords, often at "extortionate rents."

"In Dallas," Roos told the junior chamber, "landlords are free to charge extortionate rents because of the critical shortage of Negro housing. The Negro must pay or sleep in the streets." Roos said foreclosures on lots sold to blacks were common and that some properties were sold over and over again.

After World War II, black families came to Dallas for precisely the same reasons white families came: because the commerce of the countryside was drying up, the great urbanization of Texas was beginning, and money and the means of survival were in the cities, not the rural towns. Dallas was only minimally industrialized then, which tended to hold wages low for black people, but the Dallas economy, then as now, was varied and exceptionally stable for the region. Unskilled workers were not subject to the massive downturns and layoffs that crippled the ability of workers to save money in places like Detroit, where wages were much higher. After the war, many families were armed with government housing subsidies for veterans, and many other families by then had been around long enough to amass their own down payments. As the slums worsened, the pressure grew ever sharper for decent new housing that could be bought and owned by black people.

"Explosive and combustible forces are building up within the community," Roos said. "Areas like West Dallas and Mill Creek are cancers eating into the moral and physical fibers of our democratic system."

Roos' words did not fall on entirely deaf ears. The Interracial Committee of the Dallas Chamber of Commerce, made up of 25 white men and five invited black guests, spoke out forcefully the day after Roos' speech, calling the black housing shortage the single most important cause of the city's racial unrest and calling on city government and the business community to do something about it immediately.

Nevertheless, much of the activity on which the city continued to expend its greatest municipal energies worked to pump the pressure of the housing shortage even higher. One of the worst of the legacies of slavery and Reconstruction had always been a light regard for black property rights, and the city of Dallas tended to show utter contempt for black ownership whenever and wherever there was pressure to remove a black population from the path of white settlement. Establishing a pattern that would finally reach back and bite the city years later in the battle over homes around the state fairgrounds, the city had begun during the 1940s to whipsaw black homeowners out of a neighborhood of single-family houses near Love Field, the city's main airport. The city first announced that the land on which the black homes stood was to be taken under right of eminent domain to be used for airport expansion. And then the city did not take it.

The black homeowners were caught in a vise. They couldn't sell to anyone else at a good price, because it was known the property was scheduled for condemnation. The city denied building permits to improve the property on the grounds that the owners were only attempting to inflate the value of their property before the taking. Finally the only party interested or willing to buy their property was the city, at the city's price.

When John Chisum, a black physician, complained that the city was reselling the property it had bought from blacks for airport expansion to white people for residential use, City Manager Charles C. Ford answered that the former black owners were perfectly welcome to come in and bid for their lots back, if that was what they wanted. Of course, some subsequent rezoning had made the land quite a bit more expensive in the interim. He said the land in question was sold because it was "no longer in the expansion plans."

Today, the runway lights from Love Field run up to within 30 yards of apartment buildings built on that land during the 1960s and 1970s. Many of the people who live in the apartments are black. But they're black renters, not owners. That's the difference.

It is no wonder that some black families who had acquired enough money to buy new houses hesitated to buy in black neighborhoods. If the neighborhood was not already a vicious slum, it was either destined to become one or, more likely, was slated for some kind of legal hocus pocus by which the white people would render black-held property deeds into dust. But much more to the point, there simply were no new homes available for most black buyers in black neighborhoods. They had to keep renting or go out into a white world that was very frightening indeed.

When the bombings began in 1950, they were clustered in the Exline Park area of South Dallas, bounded by Central Expressway and Oakland Cemetery — an area where there had already been recent racial trouble. Police had been called in to rescue two women, real estate agents who were showing houses in the area to black people. The city manager had been called upon to speak out against a rumor to the effect that the city had somehow zoned the neighborhood black. "The city could not do such a thing legally," City Manager Ford said. But, his assurances aside, it was clear how the neighborhood saw things: The wealthy whites all had fled or could flee when they felt like it, and the working whites were being left behind to be devoured by the black rabble. There was no suggestion by anyone, at any point, that the working- and middle-class whites might keep their shirts on and learn to live next door to the working- and middle-class blacks who had enough money to buy next to them. That notion wasn't even in the vocabulary of the people who most sternly condemned the bombings.

The first explosion came in early February 1950, at night, at the home of Horace Bonner, who had bought a house just a few blocks outside a black neighborhood near Exline Park. Bonner, 57, who worked for a printing company, was asleep inside. Also in the house were his wife and mother-in-law.

A car slipped up to the front of the house, an arm reached out through a rolled-down window, and an expertly made bomb of dynamite in gelatin form, of the type then commonly used in the oil fields, eight inches long, wrapped in tape to give its shell just the right thickness, wrapped in newspaper and then wrapped again tightly in a Kraft paper bag, looped up lazily from the street, spinning slowly through the air and flopping down next to the house where it lay, its serpentine 16-inch fuse flickering red in the night.

The Bonners all escaped physical injury, but the front of their beautiful new home, the pride of their lives, the achievement of generations, had been raked and mauled and left in steaming, spitting rubble and char.

What followed was an interesting exercise in the morality of the time. Mayor Wallace Savage, a liberal for the period, took the serious political risk of insisting the housing needs of the poorest of the city's poor black people be met with public funds. But the bombing of the Bonner family posed a different dilemma — the issue not of poor blacks, who could be concentrated into small areas, but of black people who had as much money as white people, who could afford to buy and own homes. At the bottom of the bombings, Savage saw not evil or maliciousness but the predictable consequences of a breakdown in apartheid. What was needed, he said, was more segregated housing for these inconveniently solvent black families.

"Actually, neither the man who threw the bomb nor the Negro who moved into a white neighborhood is primarily responsible," Savage said. "The incident was a symptom of a serious condition in Dallas which must be remedied. ... There has been practically no Negro housing built in Dallas since the war. Negroes are living two, three and four families in small dwellings, and it is impossible to keep them from overflowing into white areas unless places are provided for them."

More segregated housing for middle-class blacks was the answer, and the race was on, from that moment, to devise just such a safety valve for the black housing crisis. The business leaders of the city began to divide sharply over the roles that should be played by the public and private sectors. Another major consideration was finding a site that would not be offensive to white people. Black leaders, who were not consulted for the most part, nevertheless felt compelled to come forward at certain points in the discussion and offer the opinion that few black people would be enthusiastic about investing their hard-earned money in land that was subject to annual floodings which made things even stickier, since the white community had assumed at first that just such a site would be ideal.

The business leaders downtown could talk and talk about building new black neighborhoods. Still, none of the talk convinced the white people of South Dallas that their community was not the intended goat. While white people with money were able to flee to the new developments in North Dallas, the working class and the strapped middle class were stuck where they were, directly in the path of what they considered the black advance.

By August, five more black-owned houses had been bombed. No one had been killed or injured, but only by random good luck. The terror among the black families that had ventured onto white turf had become thick and tangible, like illness, but they kept buying houses. Forty extra police officers were assigned to the small area where most of the bombings were taking place, patrolling each house every five minutes, but the bombings not only continued; they grew more bold.

Reporters cornered Dallas Police Chief Carl Hansson and put the question to him directly: "Do you know who is responsible for or who has actually perpetrated the bombings in South Dallas?"

Hansson said, "Yes." But he refused to say more, lending force to the already prevalent notion that the authorities knew who was behind the bombings and had no intention of stopping them. Instead, the police response seemed to be directed more and more against black people. The greatest fear of the police was always black retaliation, not white aggression, and, as the bombing terror grew, the police redoubled efforts to keep the black community motionless. In the middle of the bombing crisis, the Dallas police shot and killed Ray Butler, a black man, in South Dallas after beating him in handcuffs, according to witnesses. The Reverend Stacy Adams, a black clergyman, told the city council and Mayor Savage, "It is insultingly obvious to see the mayor of our fair city playing politics and actually endeavoring to bury the Butler case as was the infamous bombing of Negro homes in South Dallas."

Even in the face of death or maiming, all black anger was instantly interpreted, even by "liberals" of the period, as evidence of communist sympathy. Savage leapt on Adams' political association with Henry Wallace — a member of Franklin Delano Roosevelt's original cabinet, a second-generation editor of a farm journal, and the world's foremost authority on hybrid corn — and on his association with Sam Barbaria, a lawyer who had once defended an accused communist before a proceeding of the Bureau of Immigration. "Left wingers such as Henry Wallaceite Stacy Adams and communist defender Sam Barbaria have a plan," Savage said. "The plan is to gain control of Negro votes by charges such as these, that the police abuse Negroes."

In response to Adams' demand that he be allowed to appear before the grand jury, Henry Wade, the district attorney, said Adams had a right to appear, if he insisted, but, "I do not feel like the grand jury cares to waste time with instigators of race trouble and communist sympathizers who know nothing about the facts of the case."

Two months later, the bombers attacked with a fury that struck the city dumb. On one night in late June 1951, they blew up four buildings with huge charges of dynamite. The blasts were heard all over Dallas. Incredibly, no one was injured in the bombings, but, as the terror continued, it became clear that this good fortune could not last forever.

A week after the June blasts, Morris Williams was leaving the house where he lived with Mr. and Mrs. Oscar Jennings, his aunt and uncle, and four other relatives at 2311 Southland when he found an enormous bomb on the ground, a dud thrown from a car the night before. Dallas Police Inspector Dal Loe said it was much larger than the bombs that had been used so far and would have done extensive damage to the house in which seven people had been sleeping. The Jennings, owners of the house, had bought it after being forced to move from their house in East Dallas, which had been condemned to make way for one of the first installments of the new public housing construction underway at the time. And now people like the Jennings were at war. White people were trying to kill them.

All around them was the post-war American dream of babies, home, and peace. For $1.99 that summer, Ward's Cut-Rate Drugs was selling lawn chairs on which a middle-class family could sit outside and enjoy their lawn just as if they were at a resort. On the inside, homes had just been invaded by television, showing Dallas viewers a special test pattern to help them focus their sets between the hours of 11 a.m. and 2:30 p.m. (more than time enough), followed by news, the Horiss and Carl Show, Kate Smith, Julie Benell's Cooking show, and then, everybody's favorite, Howdy Doody. The ads in the morning paper said that, sooner or later, everybody falls in love with a Packard. Yet someone had just tried to maim and kill Mrs. Jennings' family and destroy her home.

Standing in her new house in South Dallas, nearly blown into a pile of splinters and blood the night before, Mrs. Jennings didn't know what to do. "I just don't want any trouble with anyone," she said. "I'll move out of here tomorrow, if someone will just find me a place to go to. I had to move once. I guess I can do it again." She said that when she had left her eight-room house on Troy Street in East Dallas, she had been forced to take $6,250 for it. She looked around the new house. "This six-room house cost me $7,500. So I lost $1,250 there. I can't go on paying and paying."

By then, the city council was flailing earnestly, if clumsily, for help. In July, the council made a point of announcing that it had asked for help from the FBI. At that time, of course, the FBI did not yet have the jurisdiction given it by the civil rights legislation of the 1960s, but that was hardly the point anyway. At least a part of the reason for the request was an attempt to thrust this nasty racial business back in the lap of the federal government, where white Dallas believed the blame lay in the first place.

When a group of white homeowners appeared before the council to ask it to bar a black church from building a tabernacle at Frank and

Lagow Streets, South Dallas Councilman Bernard Hemphill, Jr. said that the council's hands were tied and that decisions of the U.S. Supreme Court had nullified even the sacred racial deed restrictions on which whites had placed such faith. "I would like to help all of you, but this council is bound by the law the Supreme Court says we must go by. Otherwise we would wind up in federal court."

When J.B. Adoue Jr., the new mayor of Dallas, told the audience that the people of Highland Park enjoyed no more protection from the black advance than the people of South Dallas, he was greeted by expressions of disbelief. The Reverend Elner Tenery, pastor of Friendship Baptist Church at 4106 Frank and leader of the citizen delegation, sounded the muted horn of white violence. "I pray that it does not lead to bloodshed," he said. "I pray for everyone to go into it spiritually." Mrs. G.M. Purcell, a member of Tenery's group, placed the blame for violence, should it occur, squarely on the shoulders of the black interlopers. She said that, if the black people who wanted to build a church near her church "had the love of God in their souls, they would not disturb our peace." The mayor responded warmly, "You have hit the nail on the head. If all had that, we would not be having troubles with Russia or anyone else."

4

This intricate, almost ritual dance by which people invoked violence — expressing their fear of it, declaring its presence, parading its mask around the communal fires — was being played out against a very compelling backdrop: the relentless and escalating dynamiting of black homes. In public, the element of threat was always handled gingerly and with great delicacy, as if it were an infant. Or a bomb. The delicacy with which it was delivered did not change the nature of the message. It was threat.

Everyone knew, as everyone had known since Reconstruction, since slavery, that this kind of oppression could not persist forever without an angry and dangerous backlash from the blacks. It was to the deepest of white fears, the fear of black retaliation, that black leaders began to appeal in 1950. The Reverend E.C. Estell, a conservative leader in the black community who later opposed much of the civil rights activism of the 1960s, came forward in 1951 and said, "The Negro community should not get the impression that they are being abandoned to a group of criminals. If they do, they will start acting defensively." Estell demurred from invitations to be more specific, but his white confidants said later they took his words to be references to possible "shooting and racial strife."

By July, the fears of black people in or very near white neighborhoods in South Dallas had been scraped to a fine edge. Dread of being murdered in one's sleep at night, in addition to making sleep difficult, also tends to put one's nerves on edge during waking hours.

The ongoing terror induced in the black community by the nocturnal bombings made black people easy targets for a new and more mundane kind of assault — the daylight taunt. Carloads of young whites drove the streets of the Exline Park area looking for black women waiting at bus stops or black men tending their lawns and experimented with various means of frightening them. Finally, when gangs of white youths started driving around throwing huge firecrackers made to look like bombs at black people in the area, the police were obligated to involve themselves in stopping this form of intimidation.

Annie Evans, a black woman who lived on Atlanta Street, in the area of the house bombings, was out walking when a gang of white teenagers drove by her and hurled what appeared to be a stick of dynamite at her feet. It exploded with a terrific concussion. She told police she had thought it was a "dynamite bomb" and that she had been so terrified that she had broken a heel from her shoe running away.

Willie Mae Comeaux, who lived on Meadow Street, also in the bombing area, was attacked the same way. She dove flat into the curb, injuring her hip and ripping her watchband from her wrist. Before the police had taken them off the street, the young whites had hurled their powerful and convincing scare-bombs at several pedestrians up and down Meadow. The police confiscated a round bomb the size of a grapefruit, two sticks of "small dynamite" with "Grenade" printed on the side and a mechanical explosive that looked like a giant cigarette lighter. In arresting them, the police reminded the public sternly that it was a misdemeanor to play with firecrackers within the corporate limits of the city.

Already, a dual response had begun to appear. First there was the trivial response of the Police Department itself, and then there was a more deliberate action. A day after the Police Department's lecture on firecrackers, the district attorney brought assault charges against the two ringleaders, Robert Kenneth Carlock, 17, and Richard Harold Tucker, 18.

The following night, a house on Meadow where the attacks had taken place was destroyed by dynamite. The house was unoccupied at the time, but, by then, people in the entire area were so tightly wound up and nerve wracked that the blast drove panic into the hearts of everyone who heard it. James Johnson, the white man who lived next door to the bombed house, said, "When it went off, I tried to get outside. I thought it was my own house! I tore off my window screens! I didn't see or hear anyone around the house before the bomb went off." Johnson certainly had no cause for embarrassment: The area was probably full of people hacking their ways in and out of windows at that moment, smashing down doors and racing through backyards to escape the mayhem, riveted by the thought that there might not be any escape or safety. At the time of the bombing, eight police cars had been patrolling the area, a few blocks square.

Mayor Adoue's entreaties for peace had become plaintive, for now the bombings had taken on an entirely new dimension and made an enormous leap in the city's hierarchy of problems. The bombings had persisted so long and had grown so vicious that they had become national news. Adoue said, "Even a bare scrap of information might be extremely helpful in putting an end to the bombings that are blackening the name of Dallas all over the nation. Anyone who may have any information at all should report it to the officers in the interest of the good name of Dallas."

Even more remarkable than the mayor's suggestion that the "interest of the good name of Dallas" might give pause to people capable of blowing up families with dynamite, however, was his theory that this all might be the work of mysterious and sinister visitors to the city. He suggested the possibility that the entire business could be part of a scheme to discredit the Dallas Police Department. He suggested more specifically that it could be the work of gangsters trying to force their way into the city, having been frustrated in attempts to corrupt or in any way sully Dallas officials with money.

The most basic machinery of the racial peace in Dallas was beginning to look as if it could come unglued. The black members of the Chamber of Commerce's Biracial Committee were out of patience, and some white members were in full sympathy with them. A camp within the white business elite was clearly coming to the conclusion that something serious needed to be done. At a long and angry meeting of the committee, prominent white civic leader Louis Tobian said, "It seems there are some people who know a lot more than they are telling, perhaps even some policemen, I don't know."

Estell, the black minister, said again that either there would be some action to stop the terror or there would be violence from the black community. Two county criminal judges, Henry King and Bob Hall, told Estell he was talking about something that was strictly a matter for the police. Estell responded to them in terms seldom used by Dallas black men in discourse with whites. Among other things, Estell said, "The Dallas Police Department has completely broken down on the community level. They can't put their hands on anything."

The city was on the edge of chaos, and finally it was enough. In that meeting, the shape and size of what was going on finally became clear for the people who had magnificent plans for Dallas. It was all slipping away in smoke and terror. The tendency for racial violence that had lurked somewhere in the cracks and edges of the community since Reconstruction was rising, and, left unchecked, would devour everything. Who could know, even now, how far it had advanced? Were the police themselves involved? Certainly a city whose political offices had been swept by a Ku Klux Klan slate within the memory of its living citizenry could not profess too much shock at the possibility of high-level conspiracy. The people who thought of themselves as really running things, the ones who really owned the town, knew that they weren't in on it. That meant that whoever was running the bombing was raining on their parade without their permission.

It was time for real action at last. Judges Hall and King relented. A special grand jury was called — the kind of hybrid creature that was characteristic of the way Dallas already did things, a mixture of Anglo-American law and medieval practice, a combination of small-town country-club oligarchy and urban politics. Using this method, a so-called "blue-ribbon" grand jury, as opposed to a normal grand jury, was created, with only the high priests of the business community or their stand-ins named. A handful of black clergy was brought aboard to give the proceedings a pipeline to black leadership and to assure everyone that this was not a trick.

Despite all the artificiality of the process, it was a full-scale and serious mobilization. The Citizens Council intended to have its way. The bombings must end. It came naturally to Dallas to entrust the task of solving this problem to its business elite rather than to the law itself, because that was how Dallas was arranged.

The creation of the grand jury was exactly coincidental with an event that should have struck Dallas as something of a miracle but probably did not. For almost two years, neither the Dallas Police Department nor the district attorney nor any other law enforcement body had been able to point to a single culprit in this wave of terror, let alone bring one to justice. But, on the very day the grand jury was to convene and begin its investigation, the Dallas Police arrested two suspects in the case and brought them before Justice of the Peace Bill Richburg for indictment. They were an emaciated 42-year-old pants presser named Claude Thomas Wright, nabbed off the streets of Dallas, and his 61-year-old diabetic half-brother, Arthur Eugene Young, who had been arrested by Hunt County deputies on his farm near Greenville.

Acknowledging considerable help from the Texas Rangers, Dallas Police Chief Hansson nevertheless had the temerity to step forward and take credit for the arrests. The pair had been charged in only one bombing, but Hansson said, "We believe they may be implicated in more of the bombings. We also believe there are more persons involved." To which the entire community heaved a collective and inward, "So do we."

5

From his jail cell, Young continued to profess innocence. "The police have been trying to get me to say that I did it," he said, "but there is no use admitting something you didn't do. I'm just not guilty."

But Young's half-brother Wright, who lived in the bombing area, was being chatty, according to Hansson. The Rangers, eager to get Wright away from the Dallas Police, had taken him to Austin, where Wright had given a statement implicating himself in several of the bombings. He was given a lie-detector test, which the Rangers said corroborated his story. Hansson said Wright had told the Rangers that he had committed bombings in order to keep black people out of his neighborhood. Hansson said that Wright and his half-brother had committed all the bombings on the night of June 25, 1951, and that Wright had been the one who had thrown the huge dud against the house where seven people had been sleeping. In describing one of the bombings to which Wright had confessed, the police chief revealed an aspect of the terrorism that had been kept under close wraps until then: The black victims had been doing a lot more than standing around looking terrified.

When Wright threw his last bomb on the night of June 25, the widow living in the targeted house heard the bomb hit the house with a thud, ran outside with a gun and let loose a hail of gunfire at Wright's fleeing automobile. Someone pinched off the fuse of the bomb before it could explode. Hansson said he believed the police, drawn by the gunshots, had defused the bomb. All along there had been that possibility — that black people might fight back. That had been a much more disturbing prospect for the authorities than the bombings themselves, which clearly hadn't caused sufficient alarm to motivate arrests. The arrests, in fact, were not made until after black people had started shooting back and after the creation of the special grand jury had threatened the police department with political embarrassment. Only then, with the investigations beginning, would the police concede publicly that the black community was armed and shooting back.

For all Hansson's efforts at looking like a man in full control of his domain, it was clear even at that moment that the Texas Rangers were playing an increasing and key role in the investigation, and this fact alone signalled a significant shift into higher gear. The proud history of the Rangers reaches back into the very earliest history of the American settlement of Texas, even before the Republic of Texas, when horses and the Colt pistol finally gave white men an edge over the Comanches. Until very recently, the Texas Rangers enjoyed the same prestige and authority in Texas that the FBI possessed nationally. That the Rangers were even working the case in Dallas meant that the local police had been significantly supplanted.

Ranger Captain Bob Crowder found his way to the press and let it be known that these arrests in no way signaled a solution to the mystery. "These definitely are not the leaders of these bombings," Crowder said. "They merely did the work. We are still after the head man or men."

In fact, the sudden production of two mad bombers, after long, agonizing months of inaction and apparent futility, did not wash with anyone, not even with the Police Department's normally loyal defender, District Attorney Wade. For one thing, the pair just didn't have any of the right scent of initiative or guile about them. Both had served time in prison, Wright several times, for bootlegging. Even though Wright lived in the neighborhood and had an ostensible motive for wanting to frighten black people away, he and his half-brother still looked like a couple of ex-cons, losers, penny-ante thugs, the kind of people who get hired to do things like this.

In the second place, their miraculous appearance at the moment of the grand jury's birth was so utterly unconvincing that one had to wonder why someone hadn't at least attempted to dress it up with a better story. Hansson said investigators had been hot on the pair's trail for ten days and had just stumbled on the evidence needed to bring them in — some bombs cached in a field — on that particular day.

But Hansson had made political mistakes, too. Henry Wade, the smart young district attorney, had not been cut in on the arrests. Wade was angry. He said no one had told him anything about any suspects and no one had consulted him about the sudden arrests. "It is customary for police authorities to present the evidence to the district attorney, who accepts charges if the evidence is sufficient. The police have not consulted me, and I do not know what type of evidence, if any, they have against the charged men."

In this battle for everyone's political skin, Wade was already maneuvering. The police department may have had the sympathy of the white middle class, but the men on that grand jury owned the middle class. Wade said, "I feel sure that the grand jury, meeting this morning, will want to look into the sufficiency of evidence in this case and investigate the dozen or more unsolved bombings."

Within 24 hours, the pathetic Arthur Eugene Young had confessed his part, too, but even at that, Young and Wright became less and less satisfactory scapegoats the more they talked. Young's diabetes made him weak and old beyond his years. He was unable to read or to write anything but his name, which he scrawled across pages of a typed confession. Chief Hansson allowed that the pair probably were, as the Rangers had already suggested, something a good deal less than the masterminds. "We have two men who were doing bombings," he said. "We do not believe these men are the leaders."

In the weeks ahead, the two unlikely terrorists led officials to outlying fields and shacks where they said they had assembled their weapons. City Manager Charles Ford posed for pictures, grinning broadly over a dynamite bomb provided by the captives. But this show was less compelling than the strong current of rumors beginning to surface, stories to the effect that the two were leading Ranger Capt. Bob Crowder to something more explosive even than buried sticks of dynamite. For his part, Crowder only would say, "We are following up new information that we have obtained, and there will be more arrests if we get enough to go on from a man we have under questioning." Like Crowder, the grand jurors themselves were said to be convinced that Young and Wright had been "hired hands," and the question now was where the mystery would lead in the search for the person or persons who had hired them.

From all signs, the Rangers were making great progress. They were said to be "elated" with the evidence they had been able to garner, and the grand jury was reported to be looking to the "actual financiers" of the bombings. An unnamed "red-headed 29-year-old man" was known to have signed a thick statement but was not arrested.

When he brought Charles Goff, the labor leader and community activist of Exline Park, in for questioning, Wade boldly called him one of "three masterminds" behind the bombings. Goff, chairman of the Exline Improvement League, looked distinctly unruffled in his appearance downtown, and the two friends who came down to bail him out, Louis Reinle and Maury Hughes, openly snickered at the suggestion that anyone was going to teach Goff any lessons. But the reporters who were baby-sitting the grand jury out in the corridor, watching the sweat on Henry Wade's face when he left the room, could tell that the grand jury story had reached that certain critical velocity where events, discoveries and consequences begin to pile up on each other according to their own tornadic forces.

Arrests and indictments began to come thick and fast, three more one day, five another day, and now some of the accused bomb-throwers were beginning to look less like thugs and more like middle-class homeowners. Clearly, the puzzle was about to be solved.

And then, in the midst of the inevitable excitement and titillation that grow up around any community mystery, the real scope of the investigation — the places where the trail seemed to be leading — grew suddenly vast and chilling. The grand jury issued subpoenas calling for the South Dallas Bank and Trust Company to produce the bank statements and canceled checks of two white South Dallas neighborhood associations. Ranger Captain Crowder did not deny reports that Wright had said he and several other men had been paid by others to carry out the bombings. The grand jury was looking specifically for checks from the two neighborhood associations to Claude Thomas Wright.

All at once, the affair had taken a dramatic turn. If the white middle- and working-class homeowner groups around Exline Park were at the bottom of the bombings, if they had been paying hired goons in an organized conspiracy to carry out terror against black families in South Dallas — with help from the police? Who could know? — then the horse was of a different color indeed. Then, in fact, forces were at play that were much more perilous to everyone involved than anyone had imagined at the beginning.

6

On certain days, in the proper light and just the right mood, Dallas can be a remarkably Southern city, so much so that it can surprise even natives of the Old South. In many important aspects of its character, Dallas is still a product of East Texas and of the post-Civil War cotton culture. It was really after the war that the cotton business in Texas and in the North Texas region around the Dallas rail terminal boomed. In the decade of the war itself, Texas was the nation's sixth largest cotton producer, but by 1879 it was third, and by the turn of the century, Texas was far and away the biggest cotton producer in North America. Until it had been "cottoned out," the blackland prairie soil of North Texas was capable of producing a full bale of cotton per acre without fertilizer. Except for bottomlands, very little soil east of the Mississippi was capable of producing a third of a bale per acre without fertilizer.

Even before the war, then, the cotton planters who were able to get themselves and their capital out to Texas and who could buy land somewhere within reach of a railroad stood to make vast profits. While the depression of the 1840s had more or less put an end to the lavish life of planters in much of the South, planters in the 1850s were still hauling in bales of money in the Mississippi Delta, the Louisiana bayous, the Red River and Arkansas River Valleys and on the prairies around Dallas. In addition to that allure, of course, there were considerable forces pushing slave owners out of the Old South and toward Texas during the years before the war.

As the antislavery movement grew in America, both adherents and enemies of the slave system shared a perception of Texas as a special base for slavery, safe from the vicissitudes of politics and even from armed conflict in the rest of the United States. Some slave owners found hope in the fact that Texas had been an independent nation before joining the union. Could it not become sovereign again in the event of a national chaos in the United States? Decades later, Cato Carter, a former slave in the Old South, recalled seeing many "folks leavin' for Texas" who said that, "if the Federals won the war they'd have to live in Texas to keep slaves. So plenty started drifting their slaves to the West." Another slave who made the journey himself was told by his master that, "In Texas there never be no freedom."

The abolitionists, meanwhile, argued that these were precisely the reasons why there was a Texas in the first place. Benjamin Lundy, the leading light of the abolition movement before 1830, insisted that the entire revolution against Mexico had been inspired by the desire of Anglo-American Texans to maintain slavery.

Indeed, the Mexican government had attempted to stamp out slavery in Texas and had retreated from emancipation only when the Anglo-Texans persuaded their Mexican superiors that the Texas settlement and economy could not survive without slaves. The Mexicans were appalled by reports of cruelty their own investigators sent back to Mexico City. Don Manuel Mier y Teras, who was sent to Texas in the late 1820s by Mexican President Guadalupe Victoria, wrote that some slaves, hearing of Mexico's desire to free them, had become "restless under the yoke," and that their Texas masters had responded brutally.

The Mexican investigator said the Texans, "in the effort to retain them (their slaves), have made the yoke even heavier; they extract their teeth, set on the dogs to tear them to pieces, the most lenient being he who but flogs his slaves until they are flayed (their skin removed)."

In spite of these awful visions, the government of Mexico finally acceded to the insistence of the Texans that they could not survive without slaves. Leading settlers of Texas even propounded a philosophy that held that slavery was a sacred and central principle on which all of Texas rested. John S. ("Rip") Ford, physician, journalist, hero of the early Texas Rangers, espoused slavery as a principle more hallowed and indispensable than the tenets of the Declaration of Independence. He said, "The assumption in the Declaration of Independence that 'all men are created equal' was not intended to include the African race, or was a falsehood on its face."

Ford, like many Texans after him, cited the Bible and Christianity as moral underpinnings of slaveholding. "The Savior erected his standard in the very midst of thousands of bondsmen, and while rebuking every species of sin, never raised his voice against the legitimacy of the institution."

There is still in Dallas, and in much of Texas, especially among white people of a certain generation, an amount of pleasant self-delusion where the particular institution of Texas slavery is concerned. It is a popular belief that slavery was less harsh in Texas than in some parts of the Old South, even though almost every credible study of American slavery argues just the opposite. It is a popular white belief that, left to their own devices and without outside interference, white and black Texans enjoy a special and friendly intimacy today, a legacy of their "partnership" in slavery, and, based on this deep bond and the essential nobility of the white Southern heart, a lasting racial peace could be attained, were it not for the meddling of outsiders who don't really "understand" the special relationship.

A fairly complete rendition of the classic white view of Texas slavery was presented publicly in 1941, when, following a series of dynamite bombings of black families in Dallas, a leading citizen, Dr. J.B. Cranfill, pleaded in the newspapers for tolerance. In his essay, intended to bring mercy to the hearts of Dallas white people and an end to the terrible bombings, Cranfill articulated the white version of what had been the relationship between slave and slave owner and of what it all had to say for race relations in the forties. Cranfill's theory of race relations was still official white doctrine fully 20 years later when Dallas was finally forced to accept ritual desegregation of the public schools. In 1941, Cranfill told the city:

"During the Civil War, when Southern soldiers were at the front fighting to keep Negroes enslaved, the more intelligent Negroes knew the meaning of the struggle. Victory for the South meant permanent enslavement, victory for the North meant emancipation. They were left in charge of the families of the confederate soldiers who owned them, while the flower of Southern manhood was at the front fighting for the continuation of slavery.

"During all those tragic days in which 1,000,000 men died in battle, not a Negro betrayed his trust . . . . The Negro men of that time held true to the loftiest traditions of the human race.

29

"The Negroes are here to stay. All native Southern men knew that the Negro has achieved his present status fighting against almost insurmountable odds .... The Negro is religious. He has in his breast the singing heart .... The Negro spirituals with their haunting melodies charm all responsive hearts.

"There was projected in Dallas a Negro housing enterprise through which some 500 families were, under forms of law, evicted from their homes and set out like Noah's dove with no place upon which to rest their feet. They sought homes in other areas and met with a quality of persecution reminiscent of the darkest of the Dark Ages. Numbers of Negro homes were bombed with dynamite. Efforts were made to take from the Negroes Lincoln Jr. High School .... The overwhelming sentiment of the Christian white men of Dallas is against this persecution of the Negroes.

"What shall be done with the Negroes? Obviously we cannot kill them all. We cannot take from them their schools. We cannot restrain them from intellectual and economic advancement. I am pleading with our white men — men whose hearts are white, men who believe in the lofty principles of Christ ... to give the Negroes a square deal, a friendly deal, a helping hand, a kindly word, so that these two races shall live in the same environment and work out their destiny in peace."

In the first place, Cranfill's words need to be placed against the backdrop of their time, and we have to remember today that he was expressing sincere concern for the welfare of black people. But the underlying thought, that black people and white people should attempt to recapture the harmony lost but still cherished, the legacy of a golden past, was founded on a mad premise: that slavery itself was not evil and was not anathema to its black victims.

The issue of slavery, incredibly enough, still has not been resolved. There is the repeated assertion, for example, that slavery was not a principle issue of the war. In his recent history of West Texas, *Texas' Last Frontier*, Clayton W. Williams' very first words are, "Slavery was only one of the issues that culminated in secession and the bloody Civil War. More fundamental was the issue of state sovereignty." Perhaps we could argue forever before we would achieve a perfect ranking of causes of the war according to their relative importance, but in the repeated suggestion that slavery was not at the head of the list, there is an implicit dispensation from the necessity of dealing with it as a moral question. Was it cruel and evil or was it not? If it was wrong, was it less wrong in Texas than anywhere else? Is the relationship between Africans and Europeans in Texas founded on a mystical bond or on an ancient and unsatisfied evil?

There are honest treatments of slavery available in the Dallas Public Library, but a high school student seeking to understand the mood and feel of a slave's life on a Texas plantation would also come on many descriptions like the following, which is the only mention of slavery in Joseph William Schmitz's book, *Texas Culture:*

"Even the slaves had their own amusements. Plantation owners gave them a week off at Christmas time, and then bedecked & in their best, they visit each other, the evenings ending in singing and dancing."

This vision of African slaves as an essentially childlike and playful lot has continued to color the white view of black people up into the present and was the basis for the appeal of a particular form of newspaper literature presented to white readers in Dallas fairly regularly up until very recently — the profile of a hearty, stupid, but likeable former slave who is notably and admirably unlike modern black people. One of the masters of this form was the late Frank X. Tolbert, a newspaper columnist who amused and reassured white readers in Dallas with his profiles of former slaves who had survived into the late 20th century. Tolbert was a revered figure in Dallas and Texas, who wrote about his state and his people with an obvious relish and love.

And yet a young black student who relied on Tolbert's column for part of what he knew of his own culture would have found a recurring theme in his profiles of former slaves — the excellent physical condition of the venerable former slaves and the clear suggestion that, whatever black people may have felt about slavery as a living arrangement, it certainly hadn't done them much evident harm. One former slave who had enjoyed typical longevity was described by Tolbert in 1964.

"This 109-year-old fellow, almost certainly Dallas' oldest former slave, lives in a dreadful shack, heated by 'kindely wood,' at the corner of Landis and North Streets in Oak Cliff, near the Corinth Street crossing of the Trinity River. He calls himself William Satisfied-He-Done-Got-Away, and most folks who know him address him as 'Satisfied.' He gets what he calls his 'longdividity,' or tiny pension, under the name of Will Scott, which was his 'slave name.' "

Tolbert, an affable, outgoing man who obviously thought that he

31

wrote with a special understanding of black people in Texas, traded mainly in caricatures that presented blacks as behaving in ways white people would find, on the one hand, reassuring and harmless, and, on the other, foolish and diverting, as in this portrait of a rural black community called Nigton. In this piece, Tolbert summoned all of the shibboleths and fantasies his white readers yearned to believe about ex-slaves, slavery itself and blacks in their ideal state. Also published in 1964, when the Kennedy assassination and other events had plunged Dallas into the most sensitive and dangerous passage of its racial history, when Mississippi was the target of the largest mobilization in the history of the Civil Rights Movement, this story is emblematic of what white people in Dallas wanted to see when they gazed into the faces of their black fellow-citizens:

The town of Nigton, Tolbert told his readers, is "an all-Negro village, mostly farmers and loggers who've owned the land there for decades . . . . Nigton is a kind of garden of happy old folks, especially durable ancient men . . . . The thought came to me that the citizens of an all-Negro town, or some of them at least, might not like the municipal title of Nigton."

Happily, Tolbert found that he was wrong. Indeed, a man named Daddy Bob Mark, "who is tall, strongly built, with a fine brown countenance and a basso profundo voice, said, 'We're not studying about changing the name. Nigton was named by the first postmaster, Jeff Carter, and he was colored.' "

And there we have it, a cautionary tale indeed, about dark-skinned people, Africans, former slaves, who live close to nature, where, it is suggested, they belong, who are more than happy to take to themselves a white racial pejorative as the name of their town, demonstrating, we suppose, that they are too sweet, humble and childlike to take any offense at racial pejoratives.

7

People have come a certain distance since the 1960s, and we probably are safe in assuming that few white people still hold quite the cheerful view of African slavery that the Frank X. Tolbert columns conveyed. It's difficult to know precisely how much the perception has changed, since white people in Dallas certainly have learned, no matter what their feelings, not to discuss them quite so openly as they did 20 years ago. If whites have learned nothing else since the 1960s, they have learned not to make jokes about black people in front of black people. But the question is whether, in two decades, white perceptions of slavery have come far enough to bring white Dallasites into any kind of proximity with the truth about slavery in Dallas and in Texas, what it really was and what basis it formed for the historical relationship between the races today.

At the same time white readers in Dallas were chuckling over their Cheerios at visions of happy and sweet-tempered former slaves, the Moynihan Report, which conveyed an enlightened conservative view of American race relations, was telling Americans that American slavery had inflicted even more bitter and brutal psychological wounds on both its victims and its practitioners than anyone had yet measured, leaving worse scars than slavery anywhere else in the world.

"American slavery was profoundly different from, and in its lasting effects on individuals and their children, indescribably worse than any recorded servitude, ancient or modern," Daniel Patrick

33

Moynihan wrote in an essay called, "The Roots of the Problem." Moynihan pointed to the striking differences between slavery in Brazilian and American societies. Ironically, the neomedieval society of Brazil was, in retrospect, better equipped legally and spiritually to deal with the institution of slavery than was Anglo-American society.

"The feudal, Catholic society of Brazil had a legal and religious tradition which accorded the slave a place as a human being in the hierarchy of society — a luckless, miserable place, to be sure, but a place withal. In contrast, there was nothing in the tradition of English law or Protestant theology which could accommodate to the fact of human bondage. The slaves were therefore reduced to the status of chattels."

A slave in Brazil was as fully human as his owner, in other words, as completely vested with a soul and with value before God as the infinitely more fortunate and comfortable human being who happened to own him. He might occupy the worst station on earth, but it was still only a station, a temporary condition imposed on him by stronger men. But, since English and American law could not countenance unfree human beings who had not broken the law, the Englishmen and Americans who wanted to own slaves had to divest their victims of humanity itself, to render them less than human in order to seize the slaves' freedom and live morally and intellectually with themselves. This feat required the slave owner to look into the face of his slave and see no human.

Every manifestation of humanity the slave made — the mistake of exhibiting temper, certainly, but even mere seriousness of mind, a direct stare — was a challenge to the strange psychological and moral game the slave owner played with his slave and, more eerily, with himself. Thus the law according to Rip Ford, the Texas Ranger who held that the Declaration of Independence applied to everyone but blacks. They were not included because they were not considered fully human. Under Anglo-American law, the system could have been justified and lived with no other way, leaving white Americans today with what may be the most difficult psychological wounds human beings can suffer — the self-disfiguration that is the consequence of having denied the humanity of human beings.

The specific case of Texas slavery is not comforting. In spite of repeated assertions to the contrary in Texas historical literature, it does not appear that slaves were better treated in Texas than elsewhere, and if anything, the opposite was probably the case.

Energetic and willful as they may have been, the men who rushed west in search of vast profits in the years before the war, or who fled the South with mortgaged slaves, do not appear in retrospect to have been the cream of Southern civilization. In his landmark work, *The Peculiar Institution,* Kenneth Stampp writes:

"Although cruelty was endemic in all slaveholding communities, it was always most common in newly settled regions. Along the rough southern frontier thousands of ambitious men were trying swiftly to make their fortunes. They operated in a frantically competitive society which provided few rewards for the virtues of gentility and almost put a premium on ruthlessness. In the eastern tobacco and rice districts brutality was unquestionably less prevalent in the nineteenth century than it had been during the colonial period.

"But in the Southwest only limited areas had developed a mellowed gentry as late as 1860. In the Alabama-Mississippi Black Belt, in the cotton and sugar parishes of Louisiana, along the Arkansas River, and in Eastern Texas the master class included the 'parvenus,' the 'cotton snobs,' and the 'Southern Yankees.' If these planters failed to observe the code of the patrician, they apparently thought none the less of each other for it."

Frederick Law Olmsted, the perceptive 19th century thinker and traveler who observed Texas slavery first hand, was convinced that slavery had become something else in Texas, a meaner thing that it was in the other slave states. He said he had found slavery to be accepted in the Old South as a natural and inherited state of things. "But in Texas, the state of war in which slavery arises seems to continue in an undertone to the present. 'Damn 'em, give 'em hell,' — frequent expressions of the ruder planters toward their Negroes, appeared to be used as if with a meaning — a threat to make their lives infernal if they do not submit abjectly and constantly."

Olmsted said that in Texas, "There seemed to be the consciousness of a wrong relationship and a determination to face conscience down, and continue it."

A 19th Century Belgian geologist who visited Texas sounded a similar note about Texas slave owners. In the Old South, he found, "The older and most respected families have conserved the restraint and courtesy handed down from father to son. They are hesitant to abuse the slave and to mistreat the poor whites." But in Texas, "For every large old plantation of one or two hundred slaves, there are fifty small farms of ten or twenty slaves. These are the newly rich, the new slave masters who find pleasure in owning other men." The approach of the Civil War had caused these "new rich" to lose "all moral sense and political restraint."

The available accounts paint a grisly picture of the actual process by which slaves were brought to Texas. Many came by forced march over great distances, a difficult journey for free men in the 19th century, unquestionably more harsh for men, women, and children in chains. The South before the war was still a sparsely settled and often forbidding place. On his travels through the South and through Texas in the early 1850s, Olmsted often rode for entire days through wilderness before coming to the next human habitation.

The literature of "slave narratives" was gathered at a number of places during the 1930s and later by writers and social historians, as the last generation of former slaves entered old age. Some of the projects that produced the slave narratives were subsidized by the Works Progress Administration, and some were academic ventures. Because most of the interviewers in these oral history projects were white, most researchers now believe the former slaves toned down the accounts of their lives under bondage, having been trained the hard way not to say things to white people that might upset them. Some of the better interviews even contain assertions to this effect by the former slaves themselves, who admit that black people "close the door" before talking honestly about "slavery days."

Nevertheless, these slave narratives, toned down or not, provide us today with a picture of African-American life under slavery that is harshly at odds with most of the histories written by white Texans. One former slave, Ben Simpson, remembered the trek to Texas:

"Boss, I was born in Georgia, in Norcross .... My father's name was Roger Stielszen, and my mother's name was Betty. Massa Earl Stielszen captured them in Africa and brought them to Georgia. He got killed and my sister and I went to his son. His son was a killer. He got in trouble in Georgia and got himself two good-stepping horses and the covered wagon. Then he chained all his slaves around the necks and fastened the chains to the horses and made them walk all the way to Texas. My mother and my sister had to walk. Emma was my sister. Somewhere on the road it went to snowing, and massa wouldn't let us wrap anything around our feet. We had to sleep on the ground, too, in all that snow.

"Massa had a great long whip plaited out of rawhide, and when one of the niggers fell behind or gave out, he hit him with that whip. It took the hide every time he hit a nigger. Mother, she gave out on the way, about the line of Texas. Her feet got raw and bleeding, and her legs swelled plumb out of shape. Then massa, he just took out his gun and shot her, and whilst she lay dying he kicked her two, three times, and said, 'Damn nigger that can't stand nothing.' Boss, you know that man, he wouldn't bury Mother, just left her laying where he shot her at. You know, then there wasn't any law against killing nigger slaves."

Many slaves came in directly from the international slave trade during the years of the Republic. A traveler in Texas during those years recalled seeing Africans who had just been brought in from Cuba, "About fifty of those poor wretches (were) living out of doors, like cattle," he wrote. "Boys and girls huddled together. They are diminutive, feeble, spare, squalid, nasty and beastly in their habits."

The slaves he saw almost certainly were in a desperate stage of starvation, but he interpreted their behavior around food as evidence of their "beastliness." When their master slaughtered a cow to feed them, the observer said, "The Africans wrangled and fought for the garbage like dogs or vultures. They saved all the blood they could get, in gourds, and fed on it." He said the only thing that maintained any order among them was "an old American Negro (who) stood over the beef with a whip and lashed them off like so many dogs to prevent their pulling the raw meat to pieces."

These scenes were not uncommon. They were, if anything, characteristic of the Texas slave trade. A more compassionate onlooker, Mrs. Dilue Harris, came to Texas in 1833 and witnessed the landing of another ship full of slaves, these just brought in by the slave trader, Ben Fort Smith. "As soon as the beeves were skinned, the Negroes acted like dogs, they were so hungry. With the help of the father and uncle, the white men kept them off till the meat was broiled, and then did not let them have as much as they could eat."

Texans claimed at the time that the slave trade under the Republic was the source of only a trickle of the Africans being brought to Texas, but there are strong indications that the trade was much larger than that. In their fine book on slave life in Texas, *The Slave Narratives of Texas*, Ronnie C. Tyler and Lawrence R. Murphy tell a seldom heard side of the famous Texan tale of the camels shipped through Indianola in 1857 and 1858 by Secretary of War Jefferson Davis for experimental use in West Texas. Apparently, the acting U.S. Attorney in Galveston became suspicious of some of the movements of the ships bringing camels from North Africa. On investigation, the U.S. Attorney found the ships were fitted out as slavers and probably were bringing in living cargoes much more valuable than the camels they used as cover.

By far, the largest part of the slaves who came to Texas, however, came overland from the Old South. The discovery just before the war of the ability of Texas blackland soil to produce cotton created such a demand and price for slaves in Texas, in fact, that some observers predicted slave owners in the Old South would find a major industry in meeting that need. George W. Heatherstonehaugh, who visited Texas in 1834-35, predicted: "(The) occupation of Texas by the Americans ... will convert the old slaveholding part of the United States into a disgusting nursery for young slaves, because the black crop will produce more money to the proprietors than any other crop they can cultivate."

The greatest cause for the rise of slavery in Texas was the migration there of Anglo-Americans and the wresting away of the region from Mexico. In 1819, seven slaves were reported in Texas. From that number, the slave population of Texas became 443 in Stephen Austin's Texas colony in 1825, 5,000 at the time of the 1836 revolution, and 38,753 at the time of the first formal census in 1847. Between 1850 and 1860, with the shadow of war rising to the east, the slave population of Texas grew by 213.8 percent to 182,566 slaves, while the white population grew by 179.73 percent. The black population in Texas in 1860 was approximately 30 percent of the total population of 604,215.

In the closing months of the war, Texans were still buying slaves and advertising generous rewards for the return of runaways. Slavery and the slave system may have been in decline elsewhere, as some historians have argued, but the war seems to have interrupted Texas at the very crest of a slave-driven prosperity. There was little moral fatigue or doubt in Texas at the time of the war. If anything, most Texas slaveholders probably felt they were just on the verge of making their real fortunes, if only time and the war would hold away from the borders of Texas long enough.

The contemporary descriptions of the lives of slaves under this system and these conditions are overwhelmingly grim. Except for the versions recounted by former slave owners, these tales might support almost any contention other than that there was a special and affectionate bond between slave owner and slave. Certainly slaves had to behave as if they bore their masters no malice, but many of the slave narratives deal dramatically with the need for hypocrisy and dissembling, and with the terrible wrath the black slave carried locked within him.

Annie Hawkins, a former Texas slave, remembered the sham of grief required of slaves on her plantation when an especially vicious master died. "My, how we hated him! He finally killed himself drinking, and I remember Old Mistress called us in to look at him in his coffin. We all marched by slow like, and I just happened to look up and caught my sister's eye, and we both just naturally laughed. Why shouldn't we? We was glad he was dead."

Another former slave remembered being required to sit and fan flies away from her mistress after the mistress had suffered a paralyzing stroke. Dispatching her duties faithfully when anyone else was present, the slave gripped her fan and slashed the helpless old woman across the face whenever they were alone. "I done that woman bad," she said. "She was so mean to me." When the old woman died, her former slave remembered, "all the slaves come in the house just a hollering and crying and holding their hands over their eyes, just hollering for all they could. Soon as they got outside the house they would say, 'Old God damn son of a bitch, she gone on down to hell.' "

The descriptions of floggings contain too many recurring themes and specific details, such as the salting and oiling of wounds, for us to believe other than that there was an established protocol of whipping and that it was an integral, even central part of the white slave-owning culture, discussed and traded back and forth in the argot of the industry. Sarah Ashley, a former Texas slave, gave a typical account, "The way they whipped the niggers was to strip them off naked and whip them until they made blisters and bust the blisters. Then they took the salt and red pepper out and put them in the wounds. After that they washed and greased them to keep them from bleeding to death."

Many slaves fought back. Some owners even declined to punish slaves who attacked their overseers, believing that allowing the slaves to have at the overseer and seeing who won was a good way of making sure the owner had hired the right overseer. In his study of the available accounts of American slavery given researchers by former slaves, not just in Texas but throughout the slave states, Paul D. Escott found there was a substantial tradition of slave resistance. Of those slaves who recounted instances of resistance, almost 10 percent had struck their masters. By far the smaller part of that number ran from their plantations afterward. Most who struck their masters did not then run away, at least not for that reason.

Running off, nevertheless, was the most common form of resistance, especially as the war approached and especially for those slaves who were near Mexico or knew of a route to Canada. Escott found that, between the extremes of either running off or standing ground and striking the master, there were many incidents where slaves waved their hoes around the overseer's face or menaced the master under the cloak of darkness in order to fend off especially brutal treatment, or treatment they simply didn't intend to accept. But physical attacks on white people were not uncommon. An elderly black woman whose young master had attempted to beat her snatched a pole out of a loom and beat the young man, "nearly to death."

While she struck at him again and again, she screamed, "I'm going to kill you! These black titties sucked you, and you come out here to beat me!"

More than a century after the events in these anecdotes took place, the accounts of them still drip with fear, with disgust and ferocious, barely contained hatred. But this is not to say that some part of the white Texan mythology of slavery and slaveholding as an intimate partnership may not have a basis in fact. It was true that many slaves lived near their masters, and it may even be that there is a terrible intimacy in cruelty, an opportunity for torturer and victim alike to look deeply into the darkest corners of each other's souls. The slaves, in their memories of the master and his family, did remember their white overlords as human beings.

William Moore, a Texas slave, said, "Marse Tom has been dead a long time now. I believe he's in hell. Seems like that's where he belongs. He was a terribly mean man and had an indifferent mean wife. But he had the finest sweetest children the Lord ever let live and breathe on this earth. They were so kind and sorrowful over us slaves.

"Some of them children used to read us little things out of papers and books. We'd look at those papers and books like they were something mighty curious, but we better not let Marse Tom or his wife know it.

"Marse Tom was a fitty man for meanness. He just about had to beat somebody every day to satisfy his craving. He had a big bullwhip, and he would stake a nigger on the ground and make another nigger hold his head down with his mouth in the dirt and whip the nigger."

8

In a long essay explaining the Southern view of the Civil Rights Movement in 1963, then-chancellor of the University of Mississippi, Dr. John D. Williams invoked both the Civil War and Reconstruction, "The Civil war is not so far away from us in Mississippi . . . a defeated and pillaged people do not easily forget."

"Jealousy and a certain mistrust of the federal government exist throughout this country. . . . Then there is the 'Southern Way of Life,' the social pattern of the complete separation of the races which not even the bloodiest war in our history and the century since then has changed in its essentials."

Certainly in his references both to the war and to the memory of Reconstruction, Williams could have been speaking for white Texans. If the white Texan's view of slavery has become more complex with the passage of time, the memory of Reconstruction has not. The bitter taste left by the military occupation of the defeated Confederacy, still viewed as a time when the South was humiliated without cause, only for vengeance, has exercised a direct and ongoing influence on race relations in Texas and throughout the former slave states to the present. Almost nowhere in the historical literature of Texas is there any convincing argument that Reconstruction was a necessary step to enforce the end of slavery and to protect blacks from an angrily vindictive white populace.

If slavery is the most bitter of blacks' memories, Reconstruction is the most bitter of white Texan memories. Guilt and responsibility are woven together with assumptions of superiority and blame, all at this place in the loom, at the beginning of the relationship of whites and blacks as equal beings before the law. The way white people see Reconstruction now has everything to say about the way they feel toward black people.

If Reconstruction was an entirely unjust and vindictive apparatus to inflict shame and punishment on the South, if blacks would have been better served by remaining loyal to their former owners, then black people were in large part historically and morally responsible for the low station in which they found themselves when the North withdrew its protection and in which, to some extent, they still find themselves today. If, on the other hand, Reconstruction was at least in some measure a legitimate, but incomplete, attempt to reform a society corrupted by slavery, then white southerners bear a different kind of responsibility for the way relations between the races have unfolded.

The early standard work on Reconstruction in Texas, still drawn on heavily by authors of more recent treatments, was Charles William Ramsdell's *Reconstruction in Texas,* published in 1910, a period of nativism and Klan insurrection. In it, Ramsdell set out the orthodox white 20th-century view of the period after the war, including some remarks that would seem to operate at direct odds with the popular white assertion that slavery was not a central cause of the war:

"In general, Texas was fairly prosperous during the war — especially during the first two or three years. She lay well outside the circle of conflict; no hostile armies laid waste her towns and fields nor withdrew her slaves from the plantations . . . .

"The turmoil and confusion of the 'break-up', and the general dread of all that a military occupation might entail had at first diverted public attention somewhat from the most serious problem that the close of the war had forced upon the people of the South. What was to be done with the Negro? Was he to be set free, and, if so, what measure of freedom should he have? . . . .

"It had been long foreseen that in the event of Federal victory, a change in the status of the Negro would be inevitable. Indeed, the certainty of his emancipation in case of the failure of the South had been wielded as a 'goad' to a last ditch struggle . . . .

"Even at this time, despite the attitude of the national authorities, there was considerable belief that slavery as an institution was not dead nor yet doomed to die."

So convinced were white Texans that blacks could not survive as free people, Ramsdell said, that many believed it would be only a matter of time before the North recognized its mistake, reinstituted slavery and found itself, in the words of an important East Texas weekly, "glad to witness a return to a system attended by more philanthropy and happiness to the black race than the one they seem determined at present to establish." Many planters were encouraged by talk like this not to allow their slaves to go free even after the end of the war. "Thus the life-long beliefs and prejudices of the Southerner conspired with the exigencies of the situation to lead him into a policy which, certain to be distorted in reports given to the North, was in its reaction to force upon him the very things he would have feared most — his own disenfranchisement and Negro domination."

Here then we have the careful construction on which the classic white Texan view of Reconstruction is founded: that there was some sort of confusion about whether or not the slaves were to go free, with just the faintest suggestion that it may not have been a terrific idea at the time, and the assertion that it was white Texan concern for the plight of poor blacks that caused white slave owners to balk at emancipation, all of which gave the Yankees a thin pretext on which to vent their vindictive passions on the South and Texas.

Ramsdell then supplied the core of the basic thesis, which was that blacks really were not capable of living as free men and that the Yankee efforts to prop them up in that life worked against their true welfare and interests, which really lay with their former masters. In all of this, a recurring, almost obsessive theme is that the major harm and most awful fate that possibly could befall a black at that time was a thing called "vagrancy," a condition which seemed to involve all forms of travel:

"Serenely unconscious of Negro incapacity and unembarrassed by constitutional guarantees, the Federal authorities proceeded to complete the work cut out for them .... That the army officials failed to keep the Negroes from vagrancy is not surprising. The army posts were too far apart to keep all communities under surveillance, and the freedmen themselves were too ignorant to understand that their new freedom did not mean immunity from work and that they could not be fed and clothed forever by their liberators."

Finally, we come to the moral groundwork that led to the great repressions of the Ku Klux Klan — the argument that something had to be done to keep the blacks at labor and that, in many understandable cases, it had to be something other than paying them (this matter of paying blacks money for their work continuing to deeply trouble the white mind):

"It had frequently happened that a planter, not feeling able to pay wages — for ready cash was scarce, political conditions unsettled, and the outlook uncertain — had arranged for his freedmen to work temporarily for food and clothing for himself and family. . . .

"To the childlike Negro, concerned only with the immediate present, there was no difference between this and his old condition as a slave."

Apparently not childlike enough.

Into the gap between white assertion and black credulity stepped the Klan. A former Texas slave remembered 1868 as a year when life for black workers on Texas plantations had been so harsh that, "If it hadn't been for them there Ku Klux . . . the niggers would have went on the warpath for starving. But the Ku Kluxers wouldn't let them roam none, (and) if they tried they stretch them out over a log and hit them with rawhide."

The white historians who have written at length about black indolence after Emancipation often allow that a certain amount of shirking probably was understandable after several generations of slavery. What this patronizing allowance ignores is that white Texans mounted a major campaign after the war to take work away from blacks and give it to poor white immigrants whom the state was trying desperately to attract. As W. C. Nunn put it, "After a year or two of trial, planters concluded that the recently freed Negroes, having a tendency toward shiftlessness, could not be depended upon as day laborers, and they advocated increased white immigration from other states and from Europe".

Texas was by no means unique in this regard and neither was the South. After the war, faced with the prospect of free black people moving around the country in search of work and opportunity, many states passed antiblack codes designed to discourage black settlement. The most repressive were enacted not in the South, but the upper Midwest.

In Texas in the late 1860s, a major debate raged over which group or nationality should be awarded what had been the work and sustenance of blacks. A Dallas newspaper of the period inveighed against a proposal that Texas import Chinese laborers to replace the blacks, shouting, "We want neither niggers nor Mongolians — we want white men."

The European communities that dot the Texas countryside to this day are, for the most part, legacies of this period when Texas strove to become a white man's state. Still, black people flowed into Texas and Arkansas from the Old South after the war for the same reasons whites did, because the western economies were relatively strong and there was opportunity to be found. But there was less opportunity waiting for the black immigrant than for the white European, and many blacks went without work, not because they were shiftless, but because the economic ground had been cut from beneath them. Nevertheless, the assumption that blacks did not work after the war and submitted themselves to starvation because they were "shiftless" — a term that means they were incapable of caring for themselves in even the most basic, almost instinctual ways, unable to provide food and shelter for themselves — dies hard from white thinking.

There may be nothing remarkable in the currency of Ramsdell's view at the turn of the century. Perhaps we shouldn't even be too surprised that white Texans in the twenties and thirties still saw Emancipation and Reconstruction in this light, as an effort by foolish Yankees to free a people who did not deserve freedom. But the fact is that elements of this version of things persist. In the 1960s, in the face of the gathering civil rights storm, W. C. Nunn wrote, in his *Texas Under the Carpetbaggers:*

"The transition from slavery to citizenship seemed to be more than the Negro, whose experience was certainly limited, could easily make. Lacking proper leadership, he sometimes turned to crime . . . . Former slaveholders, who were in many instances true friends of the Negroes, were not allowed to give aid in the readjustment. Sole responsibility was given instead to the Freedmen's Bureau, a branch of the United States Army, to advise and protect the ex-slaves. Generally, however, the main contribution of the Bureau consisted of arousing within the Negro a distrust for his former master . . . ."

The insistent characterization of blacks as "childish" and the assignment of principal moral blame for the excesses of the period to Northern interlopers are both themes that are alive and well in white Texan thought today. In his modern history of Texas, *Lone Star,* T. R. Fehrenbach describes what he views as the worst excesses of the period:

"The state senator with whip scars on his back, now in waistcoat

and high silk hat, and with Radicals fawning in his ear, understand-
ably showed a childlike vanity, insolence and fiscal irresponsibility
.... What was overlooked was that the pistols, badges, and senatorial
bribes and watchchains were all handed to Negroes by whites, not to
help the race but for partisan gain."

Obviously, if blacks who bore whip scars on their backs were also
and automatically childlike, and if the "insolence" of adult human beings was a primary concern of society, and if all of the efforts of the
Radicals were transparently self-seeking, self-serving and cynical —
if, in other words, the efforts to erase the stain of slavery from Texan
society and invest black people with rights and franchise equal to
those of whites were all and entirely illegitimate — then white Texans
had nothing to worry about, no conscience to confront at all.

9

We will find nothing painful or disquieting in the past if we have been trained to dismiss all versions of the past but our own as self-serving fabrications. If all of the actions of the Freedmen's Bureau, for example, and all of its reports and testimony were cynical manipulations of the truth, then we have no need to give them thought.

But somehow, once viewed, once confronted, the volumes of official reports from the field offices of the Freedmen's Bureau, collected in the National Archives, simply don't ring as lies or clever propaganda. There may be some element of exaggeration in some of them. But for the most part, in the endless river of bored, bureaucratic script, looping on dully from page to page, volume to volume, the reports look and sound like any and every government missal or tally, a careful categorization with entries for date and time and entries for disposition, dull reflections at best of what took place in the flesh. The reports from Texas and from Dallas are at least worth perusing for tone.

From the "Record of Criminal Offenses" submitted to Washington by the Freedmens' Bureau in Texas for the period September 1866 to July 1867, we find a typical sampling of reports from Dallas County. These are all incidents involving white Texans and blacks who have just been emancipated from slavery and are now American citizens — the legal, constitutional, moral, and human equals of the whites around them:

A black woman named Charity was "tied up and got 100 lashes for asking Mr. Baird to spare her child, who was being flogged — also whipt for begging that her daughter might be protected from the constant ravishing of a favorite blackman on Baird's place."

A black woman complained to the bureau that her white employer had beaten her. "No provocation, incapacitating her for work for several days. Knocked her down and whipped her."

A white woman named Mrs. Cors was accused of attacking her black servant. Lizzie. "Struck her on the head with whip handle heavily loaded with lead, laying the scalp open." Mr. Menser, white, was accused of attacking Ned, black. "Knocked him down, held a revolver to his head while another whipped him."

Mr. Coleman, white, was accused of killing Kate, black: "Beat her over the head with revolver, died from effects of punishment."

The record shows that no action was taken in any of the above cases, either by civil or military authorities.

The pages roll on drearily: "Beaten over the head with revolver, attempt to kill." "Whipped and kicked, for trying to procure her freedom." "Whipping and threatening to kill, for asking for pay due her." "Beaten unmercifully with heavy club — no cause."

"No action."

Slowly, the reports roll out from Dallas, over North Texas, across East and South Texas. In Palestine: "Grand jury refused to find a bill, shot and killed her because she refused to commit adultery with him."

In Corpus Christi: "Beat her with clubs and chains — and did not pay her her wages." "A cold-blooded murder." "Was shot — no provocation."

In a separate report, the office of the sub-assistant commissioner at Sherman described the general terror gripping North Texas in the fall of 1866, "I reported in a letter not long since that all was quiet in this section, that no cases of murder had occurred for some time as far as I could learn, but since some facts have come to my knowledge.

"The freedmen here have been kept in perfect terror of their lives by the desperate men of the country, who are hostile and active in abusing, assailing, and murdering this inoffensive people all over the country for any and every pretext that human ingenuity can devise.

"Consequently the freedmen are intimidated so much that they are afraid to mention the murder of a black man until their confidence is obtained.

"These malcontents, villains and murderers are numerous and

vicious and smarting under a sense of their lost mastery over their former slaves and determined they shall not enjoy their freedom. Many of the freedmen express themselves dissatisfied with their freedom, preferring to be slaves as they once were having some protection of life. . . ."

In that sense, then, freedom could be rendered more horrible than slavery. The white myth — that black people were better off unfree — could be made to come true, but only through the relentless application of violence and terror.

10

Each of the many peoples who settled different limbs of the North American continent built its own unique kind of frontier, but the Texas frontier was in many ways the ultimate distillate of the entire westering experience. All of the reclusiveness, steely will and xenophobic independence that had impelled the Scotch-Irish border tribes out across the American West in the first place had been keenly refined by the time they got to Texas. They had been arms-bearing farmers even before they came to the New World, men and women who looked to clan and religion for their succor and defense more often than to the formal political and social structure of towns and governments.

Generations had lived and died on the advancing frontier, from Virginia on out through Kentucky and Tennessee and down into Missouri and Arkansas, spilling out finally into Texas in the mid-19th century. There were debtors, bigamists and all the array of deadbeats and escapists among them that any wild place must suffer, to be sure, and the chapters of Texas history most celebrated in popular culture happen to be the brief interludes when those elements seemed to hold sway.

For the most part and most of the time, the core of the people and culture that settled Texas was ferociously resolute and sober, the ultimate distillate and essence of the Emersonian dream — a sturdy race of ascetically religious American small farmers marching into the wilderness with guns and Bibles in their hands, a truly courageous and indomitable people, bent on holding land and making good, and daunted by not one damned thing. They also happened to be from a fairly narrowly drawn ethnic pool that didn't get much broader the longer they stayed out on the frontier. Some kept going after they crossed the Red River into Texas and became ranchers and westerners. Many stayed in North and East Texas and farmed. But they were all, by the time they reached Texas, a race.

Dallas was a creature of the more Southern, East Texan, small-farming element of Texas culture, and yet it was within even that narrow context ever the anomaly. Founded in the first half of the 19th century, Dallas didn't really begin to draw a strong breath until after the Civil War, when the arrival of the railroads made it a terminal town. A major post-War cotton boom in the surrounding area gave Dallas leverage in the money markets of the East. Hundreds of wagons loaded with goods for the rest of Texas rolled out of Dallas every day, and trainloads of cotton raced back east to the mills. The goods were not manufactured in Dallas. For the most part, they were warehoused and wholesaled there. The cotton barons of the district were not the idle aristocrats of the Old South who had disdained work and trade: They were the commercial sharp-dealing brokers with heads for business that the Old South was unable to find among its white sons after the war. They were not Southern; they were Southwestern.

Sitting at the fulcrum of this commerce, Dallas was, by the turn of the century, already established in its role as the state's broker and peddler, moneylender and underwriter, a place where bankers and Jews and lawyers and Catholics and people from the East not only walked the streets with impunity but expected to be treated with respect. It was then and continues to this day to be a place for which people in the rest of Texas often feel mixtures of mistrust and fascination. The old Will Rogers saying, that Fort Worth is where the West begins and Dallas is where the East peters out, is rooted in a fundamentally accurate perception. When Dallas began to lift itself up out of the ranks of dusty fly-by-night frontier hamlets and become a real city and place, it did so as a broker and balancer of East with West, a place where opportunity seekers kept their eyes peeled in both directions. To the fiercely determined and sober ambition of Texas folk culture, Dallas added another valuable element — guile.

Standing more or less alone between the settled East and Wild West and never enjoying the full trust of either side, Dallas developed a self-conscious fascination with its own character and origin, as if determined to explain itself. To this day, there is a lingering tendency for introspection that newcomers often wave away as simple vanity. But it's more than that. It's almost as if Dallas, deprived of recourse to the full mythological traditions of either East or West, is determined to invent its own mythology. Dallas clings stubbornly to a particular myth of the city's origin that has been soundly disproved by historians but whose persistent retelling tells volumes about the city's psyche.

It is a sacred article of municipal faith that Dallas is a city that has no "reason for being" and the city's lack of a reason for being is invoked as one of its proudest traditions. The contention is that Dallas was founded in the middle of nowhere, with no great navigable river or port or other feature of the planet on which to fix its purpose. The end of the story, as it is told in Dallas, is that Dallas became a great city anyway, in spite of its purposelessness, because of the zeal and grit and determination of its people.

A political flyer promoting a major bond issue in Dallas in 1985 announced on its cover: "There is no real reason for a place called DALLAS. No harbor drew people here, no oceans, no mountains, no great natural beauty. Yet, on a vast expanse of prairie, people made out of Dallas what it is today: the shining city of the Sunbelt, a city of opportunity, a great place in which to live and work."

In some of its invocations, the no-reason-for-being myth almost makes it seem as if the entire city of Dallas is most worthy of notice and respect as an enormous social trick — The city that was made from nothing! A brick from straw! — as if it were something out of Ripley's Believe It or Not. A not incidental attraction of the myth for modern Dallas is it fits in nicely with the kind of salesmanship-seminar motivational mysticism that always has been an important theme in the city's culture.

The no-reason-for-being myth has almost no kinship with truth. Dallas was founded for precisely the same reasons that inspired most of the settlements in the American interior during the westward expansion, because it was at the intersection of major trails and trade routes and because the people who named and platted it hoped they would be able to promote it, pull in some traffic and sell their lots at a profit.

Civic soul-searching, bleeding off into invented mythology here, boosterism there, will not be entirely unfamiliar to Americans who have occupied other small towns in other flat places. The prospect of a gang of little sheds and houses and false-fronted commercial buildings thrown up against the implacable wind and lifeless horizon of the prairie has haunted more than one novel and many of the human beings produced by those places. These places inspire in human beings a sense, sometimes buoyant and cheerful, sometimes fearful and crabbed, that the world is entirely man-made, utterly and totally a creature of will and imagination, a world view both rooted in and superbly complemented by American prairie Calvinism. And it's true that American towns come, and American towns go, and the people who live in them make part of the difference.

In most cases it still isn't ever quite clear from looking, even for the people who occupy them, whether that kind of town is bursting with potential or in a state of decline. Especially on the flatlands and in the newer places after World War II, towns often looked a little of both, with vacant lots between busy businesses and boarded-up service stations just around the corner from brand-new grocery stores. These towns are usually, in fact, balanced and teetering back and forth between possible boom and possible bust. In that terrible moment of historical uncertainty in a town's career, every expression of will and every ounce of mood becomes a mountain or a flood, the kiss of the sun or the kiss of death. The landscape is built of attitudes — a collectively willed interruption of the unseeing wind.

So in the dimension of life that is beneath and beyond literal truth, in the spiritual world where willpower and ideas and emotion and accident invent the bones of reality, the Dallas myth is a reflection of fundamental and absolute truth. All of the dust-caked, flinty-eyed farmers who came down into Texas in the 19th century made towns, and most of those towns are dead and dying today. But Dallas is a great city, clearly destined to become one of the great cities of the next century, and all of that is due in some important part to the work of the people who live and have lived there. People in Dallas can do something people in Paris cannot do. They can look at their vast gleaming city and know, just as surely as they know that the sun is hot and water is sweet, that it is they who made the city, that it would not be there were it not for what they do and have done. It is a city whose glass slab towers are made of human dreams and whose streets are paved with human grit.

Every city may be that. But in Dallas, the role of human will and imagination is the city's most central and powerful myth. At its best, it is a wonderfully hopeful and liberating myth, an anthem celebrating human potential, lavishing praise on self-made men and women, lauding their accomplishments and urging new champions to come forward and test their mettle. In its essential form, it is a myth that vaunts merit above all else.

In its more angry and violent emanation, the Dallas myth can turn inward upon itself and become precisely the contrary of its better face. Where it is driven by fear, the dream can become a nightmare of conformism and untethered extremism. If the world is a structure of attitudes and ideas, then the world can only be dark and cruel because someone has fouled the municipal myth with wrong-minded ideas or attitudes. One of the great curiosities of Dallas always has been that, for all its cosmopolitan, urban, brokering, trading nature — all the things that would seem to lift it up out of the parochialism of its surroundings — Dallas has always had, too, an extreme and fanatical nativist side, capable of sending shudders through the rest of the state.

It had seemed for a while during the 1920s as if the whole city belonged to the Ku Klux Klan. When revulsion against Klan violence finally set in and North Texans began dropping out of the Klan by the tens of thousands, many former members in Dallas said they had been bullied into joining in order to keep their jobs or business connections. Interestingly, they only left the Klan when the same kind of pressure from above was exerted again, this time telling them the Klan had been officially rejected by the leadership.

The Ku Klux Klan of the 1920s is not generally viewed today by the native white middle class in Dallas as an entirely evil force. It is a tenet of white social faith in Dallas today, in fact, partially corroborated by the historical record, that the activities of the Klan in the 1920s were initially directed less toward racial repression than toward the punishment of white men who abused their women.

It isn't easy to understand why white people should find comfort in that contention — that the 20th-century Klan got started as a vehicle for white violence against white people — but there is some evidence to support it. A typical Klan assault on white turpitude was the nocturnal upbraiding in 1923 of a salesman named Burleson who had been visiting a local woman in the small town of Taylor. The disapproving Klan seized Burleson, chained him to a tree, flogged him, smashed pistol butts into his head, tarred and feathered him, and then dumped him in the town square.

But that strange mix of xenophobia, religious and ethnic certainty, and tribal ferocity that makes up Southwestern populism could not hold forever to the ideals of white purity, chastity, and temperance when a more tempting target loomed so near at hand. Inevitably, even the glow of solicitude for the spiritual well-being of the white race dimmed as the Klan turned toward the brighter flame of racial and religious hatred. Dallas was an even more fetid hotbed of this particular kind of Klan activity than the rest of North Texas, indeed, for a time, than the rest of the South. In the bloody spring of 1922 alone, the Klan in Dallas was credited with the floggings of 86 human beings. Most of the whippings took place at a special "whipping meadow" on the Trinity River bottom.

The flames burned brighter as they burned longer. A black bellhop in Dallas was seized, whipped and then dumped back in front of his hotel with the letters KKK burned in his forehead with acid. Klan headquarters in Atlanta became concerned that Dallas was getting out of hand, even by Klan standards, and sent an envoy after the Dallas Klan kidnapped and castrated a light-skinned black physician suspected of dating white women. But, dangerous as Dallas was becoming, the national Klan could not afford to turn its back on this great center of Klan activity and loyalty. In Dallas, the members of the Klan were proud and public in their fidelity. Klan members had swept local offices in recent elections in Dallas. At a special "Klan Day" at the Texas State Fair in Dallas, 75,000 loyal members gathered to cheer their leaders.

Even when the rest of Texas had turned against the Klan and overwhelmingly elected "Ma" Ferguson governor on an anti-Klan platform, Dallas remained a Klan holdout. In Dallas, the Klan had insinuated itself, for a time at least, into the fabric of the mainstream white community and was beginning to establish an institutional base in the city. In 1923, the Klan in Dallas staged a blackface minstrel show and raised enough money to begin construction on a Klan orphanage, called Hope Cottage. Hope Cottage, later adopted by the city government, was typical of the Klan's mainly successful foray into respectability in Dallas. If the 20th-century Klan ever had a chance at establishing itself as an institutional political force, it was in Dallas.

Now, in the 1950s, the Klan mentality seemed to be rousing again, emerging from the past, and with the worst possible timing, as far as the business leadership was concerned. The whole business of the bombings in South Dallas had come at a most awkward moment. At that very point in the life of the city, in the late 1940s and early 1950s, certain shifts of capital were taking place, land trading hands, contracts being signed, plans laid, little blocks of money moving across pages to join other little blocks and become bigger blocks of money — minute alterations in the financial heavens over Dallas that would build and darken and creat the great thundering Dallas fortunes of the late 20th century. But at that point, the Dallas of the 1980s was beyond the imagination of any but a tight handful of men and women. The average human being would have laughed out loud, in fact, at the notion.

Dallas in the early 1950s was a hardshell, church-going, soberly Calvinist stronghold on the prairie, where you couldn't buy a glass of booze and they rolled up the sidewalks at night. The typical visitor from New York or Boston or Miami would have assumed Dallas didn't stand much chance of amelioration if for no other reason than its oppressive summer heat and the sheer distance it was from everywhere that was considered to be anywhere. But there were people in Dallas who saw those problems as eminently surmountable: fix the heat problem with air-conditioning and fix the faraway-from-everywhere problem by turning Dallas into somewhere.

There isn't a flatland town in America, or in the Australian outback, or on the veld for that matter, where someone hasn't entertained the same dream and said all the same things at some point. If we all look on the bright side, turn our minuses into plusses, think right thoughts, pull our weight, then Camelot will rise up from the dust. The best money of Europe, if not the best minds, will flock to witness and marvel at what we have wrought. The difference between Dallas and other places is that Dallas has done it, pulled it off in large part, and the real momentum toward that accomplishment began to gather in the early 1930s.

Men such as R. L. Thornton, John W. Carpenter and John Stemmons — the men whose names are on all the freeways in Dallas today — looked out over what others dismissed as empty dirt, and they saw glittering mountains of money, shimmering in the heat. The only way to understand the near mystical importance that Dallas places on human will today is to try to imagine all of those dry sifting acres on which they gazed in the fifties, inventing in their minds cities that they would make real through the exercise of sheer single-minded ferocious will. Every business leader in Dallas, from cosmetics czarina Mary Kay Ash to Trammell Crow, the world's biggest builder, wants to talk to you about will, about the power of positive thinking, because they're sitting on it.

A tremendous premium is placed, too, on things and accomplishments that are objectively and tangibly real, measurable in weight or number or size, things that can be counted or deposited or at least bitten. In an interview with columnist Bob Greene, Trammell Crow goes on and on about how, when you've built something, you've really accomplished something, and it's not clear whether Greene hears what is implied: that, if you haven't built something — a building — you must be a tremendous disappointment to your mother. For a long time, the Dallas business establishment eschewed abstract art with distaste and vehemence. The real, the objective, the concrete is a goal most fervently to be sought in a city that still has one foot dragging in the great yawning universe of make-believe.

Central to all of this is an unquestioned faith in the existence of an easily discoverable, objective, and transcendental right way to do things, accessible and pertinent to every situation and every civic matter, from street lights to social justice. A mix of prairie populism, Scotch-Irish frontier Calvinism, sharp-penciled mercantile guile, xenophobia, and an ultimate resort to principle and religion, it is a philosophy that elevates commonness and common people to giddy heights of prescience and power; it is an inherently anti-intellectual world view that abhors abstraction and eschews subtlety. It works, if by working we mean that it gets the buildings built, the freeways paved and the opera subscribed. It is task-oriented and totally uncontemplative.

Dallas was still wide-open, brawling and not a little corrupt in the 1920s. It was only in the 1930s, 1940s, and 1950s that a generation of white civic leaders began to meld and formulate this system of belief. Many of them were members together in what Dallas ad man Sam Bloom later said had been the great philosophical nurseries of the new Dallas — the Highland Park Methodist Church, Temple Emanu-El, the Highland Park Presbyterian Church, the Park Cities Baptist Church, Republic National Bank, and the First National Bank.

The skeletal structure of the new Dallas was already in place in the fifties. In reaction to the civic corruption of the 1920s, and swept up in the municipal reform movement fanning out over the nation's interior at the time, Dallas had adopted a city manager system in 1931. Five years later, as part of a campaign to bring the Texas Centennial Exhibition to Dallas (now the site of the State Fair), the business leadership fleshed out the city's political structure with the formation of the Dallas Citizens Council, described by Warren Leslie in his 1964 book, *Dallas Public and Private,* as "a collection of dollars represented by men."

11

$\mathbf{D}$allas' main argument for why the Centennial Exhibition should alight there in 1936 and not somewhere else was that it was willing to put up $3.5 million to pay for it, a staggering mountain of money for the time. But getting the money together had proved to be more difficult than it had been to make the promise. The prime mover in forming the Citizens Council, intended to be a fund-raising vehicle, was R. L. ("Bob") Thornton, chairman of the Mercantile National Bank. Thornton's rough-and-tumble, call-and-raise-you-fifty bluff approach to business and life formed what is still the archetype for the Dallas Business hero, quiche Lorraine and a fine symphony notwithstanding.

Born in a dugout in Hico County, Thornton and his brother debated which one was older all their lives. He mispronounced English badly and was glad to let people think they were smarter than he, as long as he won. He was all can-do and never a discouraging word, "If it's a do meeting, I'm goin'. If it's a don't meeting, I'm stayin' home." He liked business, not art, unless the art helped business. His approach to the need for a symphony ("Coldest snake I ever touched") was to say he would raise money for it only on the guarantee that he would not be required to attend. His hale and roaring manner assaulted life with the passion of a man who sees an absolutely irresistible goal inches from his grasp and feels the mouth of the void at his heel. There was only one thing that could be wrong with Dallas — not enough business.

"Hell, it's easy — you got big business, you got traffic. You got traffic, you got a problem. If you don't want a problem, go to Forney, Texas. In Forney, Texas, they got no problem, no traffic, and no business."

When he and Nate Adams, head of First National Bank, dreamed up the Dallas Citizens Council, the last thing they wanted to have around was a bunch of citizens. They wanted men who could sit down at a big table and play, the ones who had control over the money, who could say yes, make it happen and never have to ask anybody's permission, because they were the permission-givers. There were no delegates or stand-ins at the meetings of the Citizens Council. Thornton laid down the only rule of order: "If you don't come, you ain't there."

The council accomplished its first goal — the winning of the centennial celebration — and in that victory, it accomplished another giant step in the formation of the city's fundamental political style and psychology for the future. A few powerful men, undaunted by criticism, probably unaware of it most of the time in fact, gathered around like Tatar chieftans, pounded their fists on the table, shouted a mighty accord and it was done! The Centennial came to Dallas and with it an immeasurable wealth of attention and publicity. The seed of the new Dallas was a carnival, popcorn, and hocum on the midway, shouted up from nothing by a bank chairman who was half barker himself and assented to by the dour church-going permission-givers of the city. The Centennial and the vast art deco fairgrounds Dallas built for it became enormously symbolic — a loud, soaring and wonderful thing made from nothing. The State Fair of Texas, held on the same fairgrounds, doesn't belong to the people of Texas at all but to a private and secretive association of old-line Dallas business barons. The opera, the symphony, ballet, and art museum — those may be the ritual temples of the new arrivals, but the State Fair of Texas is still the closely held holy house of the founders. When Thornton bragged about it, he really was singing the origin-myth and battle anthem of his city. "The State Fair of Texas has greener grass, bluer lagoons and higher skyrockets than any other fair in the world. It's got a cash register under every bush, and we're plantin' more bushes."

On New Year's Day, when the Cotton Bowl Parade wound out of downtown and marched through South Dallas and the soaring gates of Fair Park, it symbolized a ceremonial reenactment of the birth of the new city. The Cotton Bowl Parade and Fair Park itself were sacred mysteries in this cosmology of the founders.

With Thornton's help in the 1960s, the State Fair fought harder and longer to exclude black people, even to the point of trying to remove their homes from its borders, than any other public institution in Dallas. It became the battleground where the new leadership of black Dallas was forged.

But it was in 1950, precisely when the bombings intervened, that the leadership of the new Dallas was coming to the point of consolidating its grandest plans for the future. In the years ahead, new makers of wealth in the technical and electronics industry would come to Dallas and exert distinctly different influences, but in 1950, the native founders of the new Dallas had plans that turned mainly on three considerations: 1) dam-building, 2) transportation, and 3) slum clearance. The object was to use public works projects to create value in the near worthless floodplain of the Trinity River — land where the John Stemmons Freeway runs now, land occupied now by John Stemmons' vastly profitable Trinity River Industrial District project and the wholesale warehouses and display barns of Trammell Crow, land that is still the object of the establishment's most concerted public works strategies. One complication at the time was that a good deal of this land, because it was worthless, subject to flooding, and completely unimproved, was occupied by the city's black exiles.

West Dallas, just outside the corporate limits and legal responsibility of the city, was an especially awful sink. These were scenes that are still visible in the urban centers of Latin America — hordes of human beings surviving in shacks, living on garbage on the border of a comfortable 20th century city that has shut its eyes and heart to their very presence, let alone their plight.

It so happened, however, that in 1950 and 1951, the eyes of Dallas were turned toward these awful slums on the riverbottom, places that had been invisible for so long. Through the construction of enormous dams, reservoirs and levees, along with massive sewer and water projects, it would be possible to reclaim this land from nature and, not incidentally, from the black people who lived on it, and "do something with it." But the scheme would require a massive resort to two commodities that were supposed to be alien to the Dallas do-it-yourself philosophy — public seizure of private property and money from the Federal Government.

To this day, Dallas maintains steadfastly that it never accepted federal money until it was forced to do so in the 1960s. Alex Bickley, executive director of the Citizens Council, curate to the business establishment, and spokesman for the oligarchy in matters of dogma, sat at a long empty table in the council's offices a week after the announcement of his retirement in 1985 and said, "I went to Detroit right after their riot. Here was a city that was more dependent on the federal government to solve its problems than it was on itself. I heard the statement that, 'This is out of our hands; we'll have to get the Federal Government in on it.'"

He shook his head with real disgust. "That to me was just unbelievable. We never did things that way here. You take care of your own problems! If you go back through your history, you'll find they never took federal money here until 1967 or so when they bought the bus system out."

The story is true, if it is construed to refer only to the municipal government of Dallas. But Texas law encourages the creation of small free-floating units of government to support hospitals, flood districts, and other functions that would fall under the umbrellas of cities and counties in other states. When these units of government are taken into account, especially the flood control districts, Dallas' account of its own incredibly tenacious federal virginity wears thin.

Wearing different hats, the men who built the city of Dallas not only took federal money, they begged for it. They used tons of it to create the very wealth that now dominates the city. In 1951, John Stemmons was right up there in Washington with the best of them, holding out his hands to the House Appropriations Committee. Why shouldn't he have been? The federal government was slopping the hogs then, pouring hundreds of millions of dollars out across the countryside in slum clearance money, flood control appropriations, and highway funds. Dallas would never compare with cities like New York, where Robert Moses was creating a private kingdom of federally subsidized public works projects. But Dallas wouldn't do badly, either. In spite of the little fibs it tells about itself now, Dallas didn't turn down much from Washington.

Stemmons and an entire delegation of Dallas business leaders told the appropriations committee that they really needed that additional $7.5 million the committee was considering adding to the already enormous reservoir projects underway along the Trinity watershed. Stemmons told them the money would be of great benefit to the miserable black settlements on the Trinity at present, and he also mentioned it would help to "give Dallas as fine a flood-control system as any in the United States." Indeed. The plan, when it was first unveiled in June of 1950 by the Dallas Chamber of Commerce, was directly hinged on federally sponsored flood control as its centerpiece. The plan was to 1) annex West Dallas, 2) pressure the U.S. Corps of Engineers to protect the area from flooding, 3) move the black residents to a concentration of public housing, and 4) resell the neatly dried out, plumbed and de-Africanized land to private parties for development.

The forced removal of large black populations was going on in cities all over the country under new federal legislation and rulings of the courts. For the first time in American history, it was legal for the government to take private property away from American citizens by force and sell it to other private citizens. What's more, the Federal Government was willing to bankroll the whole operation. Called "slum clearance" in public, it was called "Negro removal" when winking whites gathered by themselves. Always accompanied by great handwringing over conditions in the slums, the basic operating premise, nevertheless, was that the removal and concentration of blacks in government-run urban camps, or "projects" as Americans preferred to call them, was in and of itself a positive social good of such obvious benefit that it merited bending the concept of private property a little. Not totally unrelated morally to the black homelands policies of South Africa today, the program is still a major fact of life all over America and is responsible for the fact that hundreds of thousands of black people in America, tens of thousands in Dallas, have never owned property.

In spite of the lure of all that new land sitting out there, raw and unused once the blacks were removed and the levees built, some Dallas leaders balked at the use of government force to take private property, even if some of the property taken was promised for use in the provision of new homes for blacks. John W. Carpenter, president of the Dallas Chamber of Commerce at the time — the land baron who was already planning to build an entire new city called Las Colinas on truly virgin land, his own empty acres in the rolling hills northwest of Dallas — stood up at the Chamber of Commerce meeting in 1950 where this gigantic grab was unveiled and spoke of principle:

"I personally don't think it's right to condemn homesteads and resell them again," he said. "There is plenty of land outside Dallas where homes can be built without taking them from people who now own them, some of whom have spent a lifetime in getting possession.

"Why did Dallas not take in West Dallas years ago, when building restrictions could have prevented many of the poorly built homes which are supposed to be present now? Dallas should not remedy its own mistakes by taking by force a home away from the man who owns it. If I were one of the people who had a home, even one of the so-called shotgun variety, I would be heartbroken if it were taken away from me by force."

But Carpenter was not to have the day. After all, he had all the land he could possibly use on his family ranch north of town. For the people looking for land near downtown, the heady allure of all that river-bottom and all the federal juice that went with it was too strong. Joseph Ross, chairman of the Dallas Council of Social Agencies, urged that Carpenter look at the advantages, that the Mill Creek and West Dallas slums could be cleaned up and the land used for some more positive and productive purpose (he suggested parking lots, to improve the value of downtown property), and, finally, he made the pitch that people were making in towns like Dallas all over America at the time: He reminded his fellow pillars of the community that there was $25 million in federal slum-clearance money to be had in the deal, money that would just go somewhere else if Dallas didn't nab it.

As for Carpenter's question why, if Dallas suddenly felt such concern for the plight of West Dallas, it hadn't incorporated the area years ago, Mayor Wallace Savage had a ready answer: He said Dallas hadn't done it before because Dallas would have had to spend its own money to do it before. The difference now was that the Federal Government was dumping in $79 million in flood-control money alone, to say nothing of odds and ends like the $700,000 Dallas would be able to borrow from Washington to extend the West Bank interceptor sewer to the area, an amount which the Dallas Housing Authority would have to repay, not the city.

All at once, a very large pot had appeared on the table, and Dallas needed to be especially careful how it played its hand. Quite without the supposed benefits of removing the black people from their property, the flood-control aspects of the plan alone would be enough to create vast wealth. By the end of 1951, John Stemmons' Trinity River Industrial District — an empty wasteland five years earlier — was home to 320 brand-new industrial and warehousing buildings, with 40 more under construction. Some 200 additional firms had purchased land in the district and were weighing their options, trying to decide to build or not to build. Clearly the cookie jar was only beginning to disgorge its contents.

The entire plan depended on being able to do something with the black people. Some would be housed in the new government-run concentrations. But where would the rest go, especially those who could afford rent, perhaps even afford to buy? The past use of eminent domain and terror to chip away at black territory had already produced enormous overcrowding in the existing slums. What effect would eliminating the largest and deepest of the city's slums have?

Even before the bombings started, a desultory search for new black homelands had begun. A number of sites were discussed, always by the white leadership, often without any consultation at all with blacks. After Roland Pelt, a former member of the city council, had proposed that he, personally, would solve the problem by developing a major black homesite near Harry Hines Boulevard, black spokesmen were forced to inject caution, suggesting that, "black homeowners would hesitate to buy in a site that was subject to regular and massive flooding."

The Dallas Morning News editorialized: "The Negro leaders hesitate to go along with the Pelt site because of the lay of the land. The land is now subject in part to overflow. Engineers point out that it is perfectly feasible to install drainage works that would keep all floodwaters away from people's doors. But that will call for large sums of money on the part of the City of Dallas and the Federal Government working on orders of Congress through the Corps of Engineers." The key term there is "federal government."

If all of it could be juggled properly, and if everyone stayed calm and didn't drop his cards to the floor, this cautious hand could be played. Dallas would receive the enormous infusion of federal money, the dams and the levees would be built, the blacks removed, the freeways built, and the land replatted for development. Everything depended on precision and depended in no small part on not alarming every leftover Roosevelt liberal on the map about what Dallas' intentions were toward the blacks.

It was clear then: The bombings in South Dallas had come at the worst possible moment. The impulse was to get to the bottom of them and clean them up, to stop the noise and, especially, to stop the news of them from spreading. This impulse was a mission of more than mere ethical urgency.

It would be an entirely wrong and unfair construction of things to

65

suggest that the only interest the white power structure in Dallas had in mitigating conditions in the black slums was motivated by land greed. The newspapers of the period were full of genuinely heart-rending descriptions of the slums, and it was clear that a wing of the power structure was morally repelled by the viciously deprived conditions there. But, from the black point of view, it often seemed as if the white people were shoving the blacks back and forth across the board, from place to place, from the terrain of one white class to the terrain of another, and it was only a question of which class had more power in the end. The white people who were not rich and who lived in South Dallas resorted to Ku Klux Klan-style savagery when they saw the new black middle class headed their way. They fell back on habits that dated from the days after the Civil War. But then again, they had only bombs and terror with which to work their evil against the blacks. They didn't have banks and delegations to do their work for them.

Somewhere in all the complex welter of self-interest and principle, greed and compassion that drove the white leadership of Dallas forward, there was one quality that may well have been its saving grace — an ability to see the whole picture. From their offices and private clubs, they could look out and see the great green band of the riverbottom winding down from the north and sweeping past downtown, and, beyond it, they could see the pleasant and tidy middle- and working-class neighborhoods of South Dallas. They could add it all up. The places where blacks were allowed to live had been here, and there, and there, and now they were only there, and the great plan for the riverbottom was cutting even that ground from beneath them. It would have been ideal, of course, if the nonwealthy white neighborhoods of the city's southern tier somehow could have moved out of the way or budged or submitted quietly. But, as soon as the bombing began again, it was clear things were not going to be solved so neatly.

12

The North Dallas oligarchy certainly could have hauled in a couple of out-of-control rednecks, put them on the front page, tossed them in prison, and called it a day's work, if that had been the game, but this business was of an entirely different scale and order. What the grand jury was beginning to find was evidence of a massive and organized white complicity — not the work of a bunch of ex-bootleggers, but a complicity of civic activists, churchgoers, the trunk of the body politic.

Ironically, the unusual degree of control the business oligarchy had achieved over that body had made the business of the bombings all the more uncomfortable for the oligarchs. In the normal American democratic arrangement, leadership at least can wriggle away from the worst sins of its people by claiming to have no control over them. The one thing the leadership in Dallas could not claim was lack of control. In making sure the political set-up would be complementary to its business and development plans, the oligarchy hadn't left itself any room for wriggling.

The dual implements of a weak city council and a strong city manager left precisely the amount of gap in the power structure that the business oligarchy needed to really run things, mainly through the offices of the Citizens Council, which had transformed itself from fund-raising body to shadow government. The city council was elected at large, which meant that the only people who would ever occupy its chambers were members of the slate ordained by the Citizens

Council. The officially and frequently pronounced rationale of this system was that it would allow a few good men to think and plan for Dallas in terms of "what was good for Dallas as a whole."

No one ever really explained just what "Dallas as a whole" was, and how it differed importantly from the sum of its parts, but the concept of the whole of Dallas as an entity to which people owed reverent obeisance was quickly adopted by all of the city's major institutions and companies.

For many years, the motto of the Dallas Times Herald, clearly and entirely without irony, was: "The Dallas Times Herald Stands For Dallas as a Whole." The main use and purpose of the concept seemed to be as a caning rod to be used whenever anyone dared question the political line laid down by the oligarchy. Such people were pronounced guilty of not thinking of Dallas as a whole, and there were few more serious defects of mind than that. A person who had been deemed guilty of not thinking of Dallas as a whole was expected to return to his seat in stunned silence and ponder where and how he had stumbled from the shining way.

Some of the extreme antipathy for neighborhood or ward politics that this system engendered was certainly understandable. After all, city manager systems had been created throughout the interior of the nation in the first place in reaction to real corruption. More to the point, neighborhood politics and neighborhood groups in Dallas had displayed an uncomfortable predilection for hooded terror and mayhem. In the 1980s, the defenders of the old "Dallas as a Whole" philosophy would look back nostalgically on the at-large council system in Dallas, since knocked down by the federal courts, and argue that its chief virtue had been to act as protection against the ward-heeling politics of the Northeast. In the early 1950s, with the business oligarchy really just coming into its maturity as a political machine, not too many people were worried about the ward-heeling politics of the Northeast. The at-large system's virtue then seemed more the protection it afforded against the night-riding politics of the Southwest.

The fact was that by 1950, a system had evolved in Dallas where the political activities of ordinary people were almost automatically suspect and somehow never fully legitimate. Politics itself was suspect, according to this doctrine. The only truly virtuous public activity was civic, not political, and the meaning extended beyond the mere absence of formal partisan labels. The business leaders who sat around the table of the Citizens Council had become the city's all-powerful unelected board of directors, its true legislature, executive branch and high court. These men descended from invisible offices in times of crisis, now as fund-raisers, now as blue-ribbon grand jurors, now as remakers of the map, movers of communities and lords of the city. They were the permission-givers.

The populace was suffered to vote for or against the slate of persons whom the oligarchy chose for the increasingly ritualistic role of the city council. But there was none of this business of calling up your city councilman and telling him you were going to have his job if he didn't get your streetlight fixed. In the first place, in even thinking of your streetlight as separate from all of the city's streetlights, from light itself, you would have been guilty of not thinking of Dallas as a whole. In the second place, he wasn't your city councilman, and he didn't especially need your vote. He was the Citizens Council's city councilman, and he needed their vote.

But in all of this passion for efficiency, the oligarchy had saddled itself with the responsibility for cleaning things up when things got messy. In this specific instance, by forming a special blue-ribbon grand jury the oligarchy had caused everyone to expect it to do something dramatic. The Saturday after the reporters had picked up signs of a squabble, on the day when the delayed report was finally to be made public, the community waited on the edge of its chair. Just how far could these business titans push this? Sure, Dallas was a tractable town and these were the people who ran it. But they were confronting a force in the white middle and working classes that seemed to well up into something more huge and terrifying every time they prodded it. On the one hand, something had to be done, or the terror would explode and rip the town apart. The black community would explode and, God forbid, strike back. On the other hand, the white masses were openly sneering at the chances of poor young Mr. Wade ever getting a conviction in a local court. What would the vaunted leadership do? Go to war against its own white people in order to protect black people?

The blue-ribbon grand jury's report was released that Saturday and conceded that the "plot reached into unbelievable places." But, of course, everyone already knew that. The question was, what places? Who? Who paid these men to slip in and out of a web of police patrols and hurl professionally assembled dynamite bombs against homes where families slept? Did human beings sit in church basements in Dallas and plot the murder of children? What were the answers?

No sooner was the grand jury's statement made public than it was clear: Given the circumstances, the answer was really the most fantastic one anyone possibly could have imagined.

There would be no answer.

The grand jury would admit that the conspiracy ran deep in the bowels of the city. And then it would ask to be disbanded. After a year of hoopla, after all this terror and writhing, and after everyone in town knew that the investigation had reached into the very gut of the community, the special grand jury was not going to tell Dallas what it had learned. Dallas took that news — that this enormous public mystery had been solved but that the public would not be made privy to the answers — with the same strange equanimity it had displayed in the face of the bombings themselves, as if everyone knew all the answers anyway, as if silence and the abandonment of legal process were what history had shown to be the wiser course, as if the community were relieved to know that this ill-advised experiment in justice had been called off in time.

Sounding distinctly like an attempt to mollify contending factions within the grand jury, the report began by declaring that its work was done but went on to concede that its work was far from complete.

"In asking to be discharged, this grand jury does not intend to imply that all who had a part in these bombings and burnings have been indicted. The plot reached into unbelievable places. The acts of certain persons are well known to this grand jury and to law enforcement officers. They were involved as accomplices by confessions of those who actually did the bombing and burning." The report pointed as directly as it could without slandering the people it had just declined to charge. It said that several of the uncharged conspirators were well known and highly regarded in "their" communities, which meant the white neighborhoods of South Dallas, as distinct from the more affluent white neighborhoods to the north.

"There was evidence," the report said, "that lay and religious and community groups, through misguided leadership, entered an action, perhaps unwittingly, that resulted in violence and destruction."

If the report was indeed an effort to satisfy factions, one faction had wanted it made plain that the failure to bring forth more indictments, to dig to the bottom of the pit, was to be laid at the feet of Henry Wade, the district attorney. The report took the trouble to inform the public that only bits of additional corroborating evidence were needed to indict more "persons who had a part in the bombings and burnings.

"These persons who apparently participated in the planning, payoffs and preparation of the bombs were not indicted for the reason that the district attorney and his assistants advised your grand jury that, under the laws of this state, they could not be convicted because of insufficient corroborating evidence."

The grand jury called the bombings "un-Christian acts," which apparently caused no great offense at the time to the Jewish jurors, and closed by urging that the investigation continue. Henry Wade stated: "The investigation will continue."

The next year, one of two Hispanics among the ten indicted conspirators was brought to the bar in a long desultory trial, in which the prosecution depended entirely on the testimony of neighbors and introduced almost no evidence of the larger conspiracy turned up by the grand jury. During the trial, a parade of prominent South Dallas citizens took the oath and testified to the upstanding character of Pete Garcia, the accused bomber, among them the Reverend John G. Moore, president of the South Dallas Adjustment League. Moore was well known for his efforts to raise money that he said would be used only to buy houses back from black families who had purchased in white areas, not to bomb them. Moore had told a gathering of angry homeowners at the Reed Avenue Baptist Church, "Talking of bombing them is not going to get them out. We will have to raise the money to buy them out." His endorsement and the word of others like him in the homeowner movement endowed Garcia with an aura of political legitimacy that obviously did not hurt him.

At the time, Hispanics had not emerged in Dallas as a distinct ethnic minority. They had not yet agreed to become a "race," in the North-American lexicon of ethnic discrimination. There was Anglo-Saxon bigotry against poor and Indian Mexicans, but middle-class people with Hispanic names were considered to be "white." Garcia testified that he was a member of Moore's South Dallas Adjustment League. He said one of his duties as a league member had been to help paint "For Whites Only" signs and carry them around to place on the lawns of people who agreed not to sell to blacks. He said it was hard work persuading some neighbors to place the "Whites Only" signs on their lawns because they could get more money for their houses from house-hungry black people.

A white neighbor said Garcia had threatened him with a knife when he saw him painting a house that had been built specifically for sale to blacks. Two black real estate agents said Garcia had chased them from the neighborhood when they had attempted to show homes to black families.

Garcia's defense centered on testimony that he had been chatting with a Dallas police sergeant on his front lawn moments before the bomb he was accused of planting exploded next door. A white neighbor said he saw Garcia walk away from the police sergeant and go to the side of the house next door where the bomb was planted, but a black woman who lived across the street said she thought the white neighbor's view would have been obstructed by shrubbery. While the testimony to facts was mixed and unimpressive, the political testimony to Garcia's rightness of mind and high moral standing was not. By the end of the trial, Garcia looked distinctly less like a villain than a hero. He was acquitted.

The matter was at an end.

The newspapers noted gratefully that the bombings had ceased and editorialized that it was a healthy outcome for all, that the message had been tendered and received — dynamiting black families was not good for Dallas as a whole — and this in itself was a sufficient conclusion to the affair. That there were still guilty parties at large, that the real nature and shape of the guilt had never been measured in a court of law, that the guilt, far worse than merely personal, was communal and political, was not of sufficient concern to merit the risk of further disruption. The bombings had stopped. The matter was closed, not by law but by fiat.

By escaping the necessity of even trying the rest of the indicted bombers, let alone plunging deeper to investigate the origins of the conspiracy, Henry Wade probably escaped with his political career. It was easy for the patricians and their surrogates on the special grand jury to talk about justice for the bombers, but Wade was the one who would have had to stand up in court and try them and stand again later for reelection. From the beginning, the accused bombers themselves had sensed that they had the political edge on anyone who wanted to send them to jail from a courtroom in Dallas, Texas.

Today, Henry Wade concedes that they were right. "We tried one of them, and I think the jury deliberated about five minutes before they let him go. I think they (the blue-ribbon grand jury) accomplished pretty well what they started out to do, but you have to realize the feelings of whites towards blacks at the time. Jim Chambers and the members of the grand jury I think did a good thing in indicting them.

They almost indicted a preacher, but they didn't have any evidence. Most of the problems have gradually been solved. I think you have blacks pretty well all over town now."

The lesson in this for the black community could not possibly have been more sobering. What it meant was that the business leadership of the city, the most powerful men in Dallas, were able only to hold the organized white Klan-style violence at bay, never able to bring it to the bar, to break it beneath the law. On the one hand, perhaps, the black community had cause to be grateful that the leadership was there and willing to interpose itself between the black community and its white tormentors. On the other, the black community could not help noticing that the business leadership's willingness to become involved had been triggered not by the early threat to blacks, but only at the end by the threat of chaos in the community at large, a chaos so massive it threatened the world of white business and white business plans for the future.

The outcome, then, was not a product of law. It was a product of truce and accommodation. It was a social standoff, with the black community arrayed on one side, the South Dallas white community on the other, and the business oligarchs in the middle, threatening here, cajoling there, holding things together with political influence. The peace, as it was, was not rooted in any ultimate appeal to justice. It was rooted in appeals for mercy, appeals to the business community for intercession. It was a peace bestowed and guaranteed by the white business leadership in the interest of commerce.

And the alternative? The black community had acquitted itself with a good deal of courage in this affair. In the face of armed and organized terror, black families had continued to move into white neighborhoods and had done what they could to defend themselves: When the widow heard a bomb thump against the side of her house, she raced into the night with her gun and shot to kill. But the black community also could not shut its eyes to the eerie and massive nature of the violence poised against it.

Black people, gathered in the quiet of their homes, conferring on what had happened, had to confront this central truth of their lives in Dallas, Texas: The white families around them were capable of banding together to murder them. Neighbors whose children played in adjacent yards were capable of hurling bombs. White teenagers could take delight in threatening the lives of black adults. Yet none of this wrong was wrong enough to bring the machinery of justice into full and complete operation. The lesson to be drawn was that the machinery of justice was not strong enough to confront the problem, that the white people could not keep their own house in order, could not drive back the threats in their own midst to create a true reign of law. So, instead, everyone had to live with what was, with reality, the alternative — the accommodation.

13

There were two bottom lines in all this. The bottom line Dallas saw at the time had to do with physical results, those wonderful things made of cement and reinforcing rods that the city's leaders mistakenly believed to be bigger and more powerful than ideas. The peace was glued back together, the city was saved and the economy began its long flat race into the glistening dream. The buildings were built. The industrial district boomed. The scattered red brick warehouses, sheds, and catch-all showrooms that had serviced the city well enough when it was a 19th-century terminal town were abandoned for the enormous new wholesaling center growing up on the rehabilitated bottomlands. Dallas was becoming a market town big enough to steal important business away from Chicago and Los Angeles. It was becoming a place that wasn't far away from everywhere any more because it was becoming somewhere.

There was water — water enough for a century of growth — and land, empty cheap land reeling out over the prairie in a fantasy of potential. There was peace. They had worked it out. They had stuck it back together. The poor blacks lost their homes, lost their land, and had to live in the government concentration centers, but the better-off ones, the ones who had enough money to cause trouble, were given new neighborhoods, and, eventually they got South Dallas, too. The less affluent whites may have needed more time and more push, but they finally fled South Dallas rather than live near black people. The evacuation was swift and total when it came. The white people who couldn't afford to move to the rapidly developing neighborhoods of North Dallas, or who simply didn't feel comfortable with the increasingly Yankee immigrant flavor of that part of town, moved to little communities just outside the city: Pleasant Grove, Mesquite, Duncanville — refuges where white people could keep their jobs in the city and, at the same time, stay as far away as possible from its increasingly urban ethos.

In the late 1950s and early 1960s, the synagogues closed in South Dallas and the churches began to sell out, providing testament that will be pondered by generations far into the future. Devout white Christians and Jews gathered at the bottom of the steps in front of their places of worship with devout blacks, and all smiled together for the cameras while they watched their religious leaders execute the ceremonial passing of the keys, as if this were the happiest and most intelligent outcome all could hope for. The whites, at least, would be able to get a decent price for their places of worship while they took off for the hills, and the blacks, at least, would not be blown up with bombs in the night, and everyone would have a place in which to worship God.

That was the first bottom line, the simplest reckoning. It all seemed to work. The second bottom line, the farther reckoning still being taken today, had to do with less concrete things than office towers and streets and church buildings. It had to do with the nature of the political machine the leadership of Dallas had perfected in this process and the effect it had on the true body politic of the city. The system had an enormous political lulling effect on people in Dallas, especially people of the white middle class. The lessons of the fifties all had to do with reticence and withdrawal. Strange that a can-do philosophy should render people politically catatonic, but then in point of fact and in day-to-day life it wasn't so much their can-do anyway, was it? It was always some kind of can-do that someone else could do for or to them. Every time they thought they could do something themselves, it turned out they weren't thinking of Dallas as a whole.

There were certain things they could do, of course, certain ways to get things done. But none of them were political. None were things one could do in the open air and without permission. Instead, the route to any kind of effectiveness or acceptance in Dallas, let alone power, was the route up the social mountain to the Citizens Council and its related social appendages. It was the route of success in all feudal societies — the road to court.

To this day, the phrase "social climbing," a pejorative in most American usage, is almost never heard in Dallas, because, up until very recently, there was no pejorative sense in which it could be used. Social climbing in Dallas was seen almost as the Lord's work. A Dallas citizen could rise by making himself or herself useful, volunteering for every little task and doing anything and everything he could to catch the eyes of his betters, to persuade them somehow that he was a cut above, was leadership can-do material.

It was all very agonizing and claustrophobic. None of it was political, because politics was evil. All of it was based on virtue and on the ability of the permission-givers to recognize virtue. It went without saying: None of it had a damned thing to do with black people.

As for the possibility that any of what the business leadership did was self-interested, there is no giving of ground on that point by the oligarchy, even today. There is no compromise where virtue is concerned. Alex Bickley, the recently retired director of the Citizens Council, said: "To assume that a person who is head of a business is doing things for business reasons is completely wrong. The things John Stemmons does, he doesn't do for business reasons, he does for people reasons. He's really interested in folks.

"Thornton — his motivation was to make a great community where everybody benefits. I don't know of anybody that I've ever worked with from the business community that did the work they did for the minority community from a selfish standpoint."

Of course, none of that was the point at the time. The point, as Dallas scraped past the threat of the bombings, was that, in the process of scraping, it had developed an effective and pragmatic way of getting things done and a definite and idiosyncratic political structure. The arrangement may have been a tight fit for them, but, to their credit, the oligarchs were seldom interested in wriggling out of responsibility. They were too busy exercising control. At no time since its creation had the increasingly formal and institutionalized machinery of oligarchy served the business leadership of Dallas so well in the exercise of control as it had in 1950 and 1951.

The accommodation also had one direct and tangible benefit for blacks in Dallas beyond the simple cessation of the bombing. The white leadership of the community, with major financial help from businesmen Karl Hoblitzelle, Fred Florence, John E. Mitchell, Jr., J.

L. Latimer, and homebuilder Jerome Crossman, agreed to provide space for an entirely new neighborhood of brand-new homes, far from the slums, for occupation by the emerging black middle class. The black middle class, after all, with its ability to afford good housing, was viewed as the source of the problem in the first place. The new neighborhood was named for Dr. R. T. Hamilton, a black physician who had been an influential member of the first biracial committee organized after the 1940 bombings.

The plan for an entire new neighborhood was an evolution, albeit much grander and perhaps even more enlightened, of the buy-outs that had followed the bombings of the 1940s, when the city had purchased houses from black homeowners in white neighborhoods. In this case, no one was being forced to sell or to move, but the alternative of a neighborhood free from hatred and bombing was obviously attractive to many black families, even if the neighborhood was to be completely segregated.

So Hamilton Park was born, a black middle-class ghetto in the middle of what was then acres and acres of gently rolling empty land between North Dallas and the small town of Richardson. Hoblitzelle's chain of movie theatres would resist racial integration in the 1960s; Fred Florence alarmed the city's more cosmopolitan populace in the 1960s when he sided briefly with ultrarightists who wanted to ban "communist" art from the Dallas Museum of Fine Arts; but, in the creation of Hamilton Park, men such as Florence, Hoblitzelle, and others acted in good conscience and on what was, for their day and place, liberal conviction. This was part of the deal. The city's business leadership might not be able to bring the conspirators to justice behind the wave of bombing terror in South Dallas, but it would do what it could to balance the wrong. For example, in deciding who would be able to move into the new ghetto, and who would not, the white sponsors gave special preference to black families being pushed out of the Love Field area by the city.

The black middle class of Dallas did what middle-class people of all colors and all places were doing in the fifties: It opted for home, family, and security, even if the deal meant turning its back on the poor black people who were left behind in the ever more squalid ghettos and in the rank after rank of bleak new public housing blocks being built.

By the late 1960s, the philosophical and historical basis for Hamilton Park had already faded, and the phenomenon of black families living a segregated life on land and in houses designed and arranged for them by white people was less acceptable in the black community at large than it had been in the early 1950s. A black South Dallas resident said in 1967, "Hamilton Park is a massive ghetto, a clique as self-satisfied as Highland Park. The people who are not long gone from South Dallas still have contact with friends and relatives here, but in another generation they will have no relation to other parts of Dallas."

Now in the 1980s, Hamilton Park is the object of a real estate phenomenon called the "neighborhood buyout." Upscale white neighborhoods and valuable commercial development have pushed in around the pleasant brick ranch-style homes of Hamilton Park, enormously inflating the value of the land, and developers have attempted to buy the entire neighborhood as a single parcel. The prices offered have been so high that many families in Hamilton Park have been tempted to organize a neighborhood-wide deal with the developers. But the terms of deal include the provision that all of the people in Hamilton Park must sell at once and together.

The putative reason why a developer would want to buy the entire neighborhood, instead of some part of it, is that the developer would have an easier time getting the land rezoned to more valuable uses if there were no neighbors left to object. But the political unpopularity of such deals with a more growth-wary city council suggests another motive for the continued interest in buying, not part, but all of Hamilton Park. By buying out every family, they would eliminate the black presence in the area.

However those factors may operate now and whatever role Hamilton Park may play today in the larger city, it was a heaven for the black families moving into the just-completed houses in May of 1954. The word they used was "dream." On that day, looking up from the boxes, urging her husband to go easy with the family crystal, Mrs. Elgin Thomas said, "It's a dream, all right."

The dream, of course, was the American dream — a new house, a beautiful lawn on which one could place lawn chairs from Ward's Cut-Rate Drugs, a place where one could fall in love with a Packard, watch Howdy Doody, and do all the things the rest of middle-class America did instead of living in relentless fear. The fact that it was all brand-new was especially heady. Donald Payton, a historian on the staff of the Dallas Historical Society, was one of a generation of blacks who grew up in Hamilton Park. Its special magic and meaning are still strong in his memory.

In the Payton household, as in many Hamilton Park families, everyone worked. His father worked for the Post Office and his mother cleaned houses, but adults in Hamilton Park almost always had second jobs and teenagers worked after school and during vacations. Except for some positions in the professions, Dallas in the early 1950s did not offer employment for blacks in truly middle-class jobs, so the residents of Hamilton Park made their house payments by becoming members of a kind of super-working class. The price in effort was worth the reward, Payton said.

"In middle-class South Dallas, you had to move into the houses that the upper middle-class Jewish families had lived in on South Boulevard, Park Row and so on. In that whole period of the fifties, Hamilton Park was completely different, because Hamilton Park was all brand-new.

"On Saturday evenings, there was a virtual parade of cars coming up through there — people, black folks, wanted to see black folks with brand-new houses, brand-new streets, manicured lawns. Hamilton Park had teachers, lawyers, doctors, and you had people that were just ordinary working people, but it gave us that sense of community, of pride that all communities have to have to exist, that all cities have to have to exist, and, as a result, they took special care to keep Hamilton Park spotless. It removed us from racial tensions that Dallas was feeling in South Dallas at the time. It gave Dallas and the fathers of Dallas a liberal look, because they had sat down at a table with Dallas' leading blacks and had come up with a plan for adequate housing."

Hamilton Park was segregated, but somehow its isolation in the middle of nowhere softened that reality. Payton said, "We were totally separate from the white community, but it was just like we were on an island. The only surroundings were woods and little rural towns, a little place over there called Vickery that's no longer there (now the locus of the Upper Greenville Avenue singles scene), and Plano and Richardson (now booming, mainly white Sunbelt transplant settlements). Those were just farm towns."

Payton attended Hamilton Park's all-black 12-room school, from first grade through the end of high school. The school, now part of the Richardson Independent School District, is the site of a special "pacesetter" program devised to satisfy federal desegregation standards.

There were no stores, theatres or restaurants for black people in or near Hamilton Park. For those amenities, the residents had to drive into Dallas, often to the "Short North Dallas" neighborhood at Hall and Thomas. "Anything we had to do, we had to come into Dallas, and that was still segregated. We'd usually go to the Thomas and Hall area, where there were restaurants, movie theatres, a swimming pool, barbershops." Short North Dallas — the "Freedmen's Town" where blacks first owned land in the city after the Civil War — is now almost entirely bulldozed and awaiting the final stages of high-rise upscale redevelopment and gentrification.

Home was always the center of life and a source of deep and powerful pride for the residents of Hamilton Park. In this entire saga — the bombings, the grand jury, the creation of Hamilton Park — a lesson from the days just after Emancipation was rediscovered and re-learned. In the first years after Emancipation, many black people moved to Texas because land there was cheap and available and because Texas was far away from their former masters. Ironically, some of the inhabitants who had had to make way for the new Hamilton Park development were black families who had lived just such isolated lives on that ground since the Civil War. Like them, the blacks who founded many of the small black towns of rural East Texas had ordered their lives on the principle that the best life was the one farthest away from white people. Hamilton Park, a wonderfully happy place for most of its residents, was a reliving and a reinforcement of the same principle.

Payton said, "The high point was on Saturday morning. There used to be 80, 90 people out on a Saturday morning cutting their yards. The conditions changed because people integrated. Suburbia started to build up, Richardson started to build, Far North Dallas started to build. From my generation up, people started to expand their borders, go off to college, move out of Hamilton Park.

"But that same sense of pride is still there. That's why, when the developers came out, some people turned down a quarter of a million dollars, because they said they just didn't want to sell, because, wherever they went, they were not going to have what they had in Hamilton Park. They weren't going to have the neighborhood sense of pride. They weren't going to have that community tradition, neighbors, friends, loved ones, people they had been living next door to for 30 years.

"You're talking about people who lived and died paying for those houses. If they moved in in '55, they're just paying off those loans now. A lot of those men, working two jobs, died and left widows and families. You know, again, that was their sense of pride. Money can't buy a sense of pride, money can't buy community respect."

Many of the people who were destined to become leaders in the black community in Dallas today grew up and learned what they knew of the world in this setting. Much of what they knew was that, in their case anyway, in their lives, happiness had occupied an inverse relationship with proximity to white people. Peace and happiness were things black people found in their own midst. Happiness was separation — separation from whites, which was certainly understandable, and separation from the rest of the black community, which was unfortunate.

Payton said, "When we accepted integration, we traded the best of what we had for almost the worst of what lower- middle-class whites had."

14

Texas has always been unique and separate from the national culture, and Dallas, in its not always very comfortable role as broker of money and fashion between Texas and the world beyond, has always been a changeling, gregarious and outward-bound in one chapter of its life, suspicious and rigid, inward and fearful in the next, tugged on one side by the xenophobic impulses of the state and on the other by the lure of the great beyond. Dallas has had a long on-again-off-again passion for New York and the outside world, for which Dallas has always felt guilty.

By the late 1950s, the passion was off again. The events of the early 1950s had helped impel Dallas into one of its deepest retreats from national reality. Part of the lesson, after all, had been that great danger lurked in the hearts of ordinary men, danger capable of upsetting all the best laid plans of the leadership. Another part of the lesson had been that, left to its own devices and unbothered by outside influence, Dallas seemed to be able to take care of itself. It had taken a vast amount of federal money to get things set up for the big play, but, thank goodness, it had been the kind of federal money you don't have to do much to deserve, at least not in terms of meeting some kind of guidelines or standards. All of the money from Washington had been socked into nice physical things, large things, highways, levees, dams, dirt, water. It's pretty hard to attach strings to a dam. What are they going to do, take part of it back? No. Even the money from Washington had been used to help fortify Dallas against outside control, even against Washington itself. Very neatly done. In the meantime, there certainly seemed to be grim forces moving on the national horizon that any businessman with his eye on the main chance would be eager to avoid. Dallas saw the future, and the future was within.

Many of the popular nightspots and eateries where Dallasites had rubbed shoulders with visiting firemen for a generation, like the popular Mural Room in the Baker Hotel downtown, closed their doors to the public in the fifties and became private clubs. Of course now, in the 1980s in a world that is all too tied together and accessible by cellular telephone, the business executives' desire for privacy is epidemic everywhere. But in the 1950s, in Dallas, the urge for privacy was not an altogether benign dynamic. The men who gathered in private clubs for the typically early and relatively brief Dallas business luncheon were not especially disposed toward extremism in the form of extreme individualism, but they may have been of a sort that was susceptible to extreme conformism.

The Dallas business establishment had never been dominated or even importantly influenced by oilmen or land barons. Nobody really cares much about an oilman's politics, as long as his oil is made out of oil. But loan officers and trust managers, insurance salesmen and clothing buyers, house builders and land-flippers: The men and very few women who really ran Dallas in the 1950s were people whose fortunes were made in society, not in the stuff of the earth. The great irony of their lives was that, for all their worship of things concrete, the lives and careers of the leaders of Dallas had to be played out in the evanescent realm of social abstraction, cooperation, acceptance, and right-mindedness. All the more reason to define the rules closely: If what we're about is all a creature of mind, then let's be very certain to keep our minds right. In the best of times for Dallas, this municipal bent has made the city genuinely special and interestingly unlike mainstream American culture. In the worst of times, the same tendency has made the city subject to a kind of moral and intellectual implosion.

The beyond, what was outside, was looking awfully frightening just then. Just as the leadership felt it had quelled the threat of violent disruption from within, a much larger threat began to appear on the borders, and very few white people in Dallas could figure out why. The only way to understand the absolute randomness and unrelatedness that the events of the period assumed in the white city's eye is to remember that, for the most part, white people of the period had not come to any real moral or intellectual awareness of how black people thought or felt. The distortion of reality that the white race had inflicted on itself in order to countenance the horror of slavery was still very much at play. In the white view, black people were happy. They were childlike. They were simple. They were at best earthy, at worst, feral. They were not fully human.

Given this self-imposed interruption of reality, it was not possible for the average white to see the linear and relentless sameness of the black struggle — that black people had never swerved an inch from their progress, from the first hoe raised to drive back a beating to the moment of lighting out, before or after Emancipation, through Reconstruction and the early 19th century, the formation of the Progressive Voters Leagues in the 1930s, the move out into the white neighborhoods in the 1940s and 1950s. Nothing had changed, not ever, not anywhere, in the South or the North. From the beginning, black people had sought one thing — every single thing white people had.

In white eyes, the eruptions of the 1950s were random, inexplicable, either coincidence or the work of plotters. Of course, it was difficult — not impossible, just difficult — to blame the decisions of the United States Supreme Court on plotters. On May 17, 1954, when the nine robed judges strode to their leather chairs at the long mahogany bench and handed down the most momentous decision for American society since Dred Scott in 1857, it was states' rights advocate Chief Justice Earl Warren who read the court's opinion.

Brown v. Board of Education of Topeka didn't leave much room for doubt. It said: "We conclude that in the field of public education the doctrine of 'separate but equal' has no place." That should have been clear. The court was saying that formal segregation in education and inevitably in the other public arenas of life was unconstitutional. But for a long time white people all over America kept looking for paragraphs or phrases, a dispensation that might say something like, "... except for Arkansas," or, "Of course this doesn't include the Pinkston School in West Dallas."

Now, looking back on the 1950s, white Dallasites tend to say Dallas had always taken segregation very much for granted without really thinking about its origins or doing anything special to perpetuate it. By this version of things, segregation was just there, an inherited aspect of reality. Black Dallasites remember something more active and aggressive.

Over the years, Dallas had worked out a number of arrangements designed to ensure that even the old separate but equal business wouldn't be burdensome on whites. In the 1950s, the Park Cities and other surrounding white suburbs and towns, rather than go to all the bother of actually building schools of any sort for black students, let alone provide "equal" ones, told black students who wanted to go to school to attend the black schools in Dallas. Dallas School Superintendent W. T. White defended the practice as an "accommodation." Black parents were finally able to get it overturned, not on any constitutional basis but as a violation of Texas' own segregation laws. Highland Park alderman C. K. Bullard suggested in reaction to the ruling that the city might have to ask its residents to fire all of their black live-in employees rather than be forced to build schools for them, but, by then of course, events were rushing far beyond even Mr. Bullard's worst fears.

Whatever the prescription might have been on paper, the way it had worked out in Dallas was strong on the separate and very light on the equal. The signs on the buses that designated some seats as "Colored" and others "White" were movable, but somehow no matter what the ratio of black to white might have been on board, the signs never moved up beyond the middle of the bus. Except for a few all-black buses like the State Street line, halfway was the magic mark, no matter what, so that there were often black people standing and wedged together in the back while there were empty seats up front. For blacks, the restaurants weren't equal: They were just closed. There were also all the myriad ways in which the system, even when it did admit blacks, worked to humiliate them.

Eddie Bernice Johnson came to Dallas in 1956 right after nursing school at Notre Dame. She had grown up in Waco, which was strictly segregated, but she still remembers that segregation in Dallas in the 1950s had a special bite. "In Waco, I had never witnessed the kind of extreme separatism I did here. In Waco they had 'Colored' and 'White' signs all over, and there was a history of lynchings. But, in Dallas, the overt racism immediately became very clear."

Ms. Johnson, who went on to become a state legislator and later received a federal appointment from President Jimmy Carter, was a tiny 20-year-old when she showed up to accept the nursing position she had been offered at the Dallas Veterans Hospital. "I had just finished nursing school in South Bend. My father worked for the V.A. in Waco, and two members of the same family couldn't work for the

86

same federal facility, so I applied for a position in Dallas, and they accepted me.

"When I showed up, they were shocked that I was black. They hadn't had any black professionals at all at that time in Dallas. Suddenly all the nurses residences were 'full' and the rest were 'under construction.' I found housing in a rooming house. That was very prevalent among blacks, because there were very few apartment buildings."

She got her first real feel for the special nature of segregation in Dallas that summer, when she was called back to South Bend to attend a friend's wedding. "I was going by train, and I wanted a small collapsible hat to put on my head. We were always raised to buy quality. My parents taught us that, even if you couldn't buy much, you should buy the best, so I went to one of the best stores downtown, A. Harris. And I was told that I could not try on hats or shoes. They had to measure my head and then go over and measure the hat."

Blacks who wanted to buy clothing in the stores downtown during the 1950s could not try anything on. Nothing that had touched the skin of a black person could be sold to a white person. The message for black people was that white people not only wanted to be separate from them but found their skin dirty and loathesome.

"That was the first real realization. I had never experienced anything like that, even in Waco. But it was that way everywhere in Dallas. Volk Brothers wouldn't even let you flip through their dresses on the rack. They escorted you to a dressing room and brought you whatever you wanted to see." Eddie Bernice Johnson, nevertheless, was bound and determined that when she bought clothes she would buy the best anyone had to sell in Dallas. She made friends with a white woman whom she remembers well to this day, a salesperson at Neiman-Marcus who worked in a special sports department tucked away in a corner of the old downtown store, accessible from the street by a separate entrance, where the cosmetics department is today. "When she was there and I went in, everything was normal."

In the 1960s, Eddie Bernice Johnson would help organize the first black boycotts of downtown stores to force them to open up their shelves and employment to blacks. Later, she was only able to run for the Legislature — impossible for a federal employee under the Hatch Act — because Stanley Marcus gave her a job with the store on the condition that she run.

Other cities in the nation were every bit as riven by caste and loathing as Dallas, and white Dallas couldn't help noticing it was precisely those cities, its spiritual sister cities, that seemed most prone to come apart at the seams under the strange pressures of the period. Where on earth was it all coming from? In the rest of the country, all manner of inexplicable forces were afoot in the night. A group of blacks who thought they were superior to white people, called the Black Muslims, was growing rapidly in the summers of 1954 and 1955. White people all over the South were talking about impeaching the Chief Justice of the Supreme Court, arguing that he was a subversive plotter.

On December 1, 1955, Rosa Parks boarded a bus in Montgomery, Alabama and decided that she would not sit in the colored seats. Her refusal certainly was not the first time a black American had simply had enough and refused to play the game. Police cars had swarmed through the night in Dallas in the early 1940s when a group of black bus riders suddenly refused to obey the rules and threatened the bus driver with violence if he tried to make them obey. On another occasion, a black bus rider in Dallas was accused of losing his temper and threatening a driver with a knife when the driver refused to move the "Colored" sign so that black people could sit. In fact, black people never accepted the arrangement in peace, they accepted it with bitterness and wrath. It was that bitterness that gave segregation everywhere its ongoing and relentless undercurrent of violence: The final snap was never far, the anger was never gone.

But, in 1955 when Rosa Parks took her seat in the white section of the bus in Montgomery, it was, as Eldridge Cleaver put it years later, one of those magic moments in history when, "somewhere in the universe a gear in the machinery had shifted." A 26-year-old Harvard graduate and Ph.D. named Martin Luther King took up her cause and led a black boycott of the bus system, battling toe-to-toe with Montgomery Mayor W. A. Gayle and the White Citizens Council. Spring and summer passed, and the boycotters were not only still resolute: They were winning. By the time a Supreme Court decision outlawing segregation of transportation brought the matter to a close, the Montgomery boycott had galvanized black resistance all over the country, had made a national figure of King and, what certainly did not go unnoticed in Dallas, had made goats of the white leadership of Montgomery.

Then it was happening all at once and everywhere. The white citizens of Greenwood, Mississippi were presented to the world as barely human savages in the murder of a 14-year-old Chicago boy named Emmett Till. When 12 black students prepared to enroll in the white schools in Clinton, Tennessee, the night-riding white mob was not quelled before authorities had brought to bear 100 state troopers, 633 National Guardsmen and seven M-41 tanks.

As each new Supreme Court decision fell and the long months of aftermath crawled by, Dallas remained calm for the most part, but the violence crept closer every day. The men in the clubs at the tops of the towers had only to lift their eyes up off the riverbottom where their plans were laid, out beyond the beckoning acres where they saw whole new cities rising, and they could see it.

In September 1956, when Texas Governor Allan Shivers was still talking about "interposition" and other delusions of the die-hard segregationists, explosive racial violence struck the little town of Mansfield, a community of 1,450 south of Fort Worth. Three black students were slated to join 300 whites in the local schools but withdrew after 400 men burst into the school waving placards at them saying, "Dead Coons Are the Best Coons" and "$2 A Dozen For Nigger Ears." Two effigies of hanged blacks dangled over the front of the school, and the school principal said,"Yes, they might be there until Christmas. I'm not taking them down." Angry men in trucks chased Associated Press reporter Irwin Frank out of town and ran him off the road. They told him the whole catastrophe was the work of outsiders like him. "It's the outsiders stirring up this trouble. It's the NAACP getting these little nigger kids to register."

If only it could have been true, if only these explosions of violence and intimidation were really the work of some foreign agency, sunspots, fluoride, anything outside the city, then Dallas would know just what to do: Pull up the bridge and boil the oil! But the black community in Dallas made certain no one would think it could be that easy. While the embattled blacks out in the rural towns and counties were trying to get their children enrolled in school, black leaders in Dallas were insisting on that and much more: In 1955, C. B. Bunkley Jr. and Frank W. Phillips, both black, announced they would run for seats on the school board. Bunkley, a native of Denison and a University of Michigan Law School graduate, and Phillips, president of his own business school in Dallas for 25 years, clearly were able men, both known and respected in the white and black communities, clearly serious in their intent. Their candidacies were headed nowhere under the existing political framework, but their boldness in standing for office served notice that the black community of Dallas wanted everything black communities anywhere else in America wanted. There weren't going to be any hidden paragraphs or secret codicils giving Dallas a dispensation.

The events in Little Rock in 1957 gave Dallas special pause. There, city officials had hoped to squeak through the integration of Central High School with as little hoopla as possible. Mayor Woodrow W. Mann had led Little Rock's city fathers in devising a careful seven-year desegregation plan, handpicking the black students who would lead the way and carefully choreographing each step in advance. But Governor Orval Faubus, faced with a stiff battle for reelection against two racists, sent the National Guard in at 9 p.m. on September 2, 1957. The guard set up a perimeter around the high school with fixed bayonets, and all at once all the best intentions and plans of the mayor and his responsible friends were out the window, and Little Rock was destined for infamy. With this ugly picture so near at hand, Texas' new governor, Price Daniel, who had distinct leanings toward racist demagoguery himself, was no great comfort to Dallas.

15

The permission-givers of Dallas could count on their ability to control almost but not quite everyone who had power in Dallas. Clergy, for example, had their own independent accesses to power, and one of the most influential was W. A. Criswell, whose First Baptist Church downtown was even then the biggest Baptist congregation in the country and he himself, not incidentally, already one of the most influential national figures in conservative Baptist circles. Criswell, still pastor of First Baptist today, gave the invocation at the Republican National Convention in Dallas in 1984. He has moderated his views on integration since the 1950s.

In 1956, some months before the terrible outbreak of violence in Mansfield, Criswell had shocked even conservative Baptists in America with two fiery segregationist speeches delivered in South Carolina but reported around the country. Criswell, in South Carolina to address the annual Baptist Conference on Evangelism at Columbia, gave gatherings of Baptists and politicians there a taste of the kind of stem-winding, Bible-thumping, Texas stump oratory that was setting his congregation on fire back in Dallas. The effect in South Carolina, rather than delight, was shock.

Criswell told his audiences that racial segregation wasn't enough. He wanted religious segregation, too. He warned that integration of all kinds was the work of "outsiders" who, if unchecked, would "get in your family." He urged people of different religious persuasions to "stick to their own kind." The speeches were replete with oblique references to physical loathing: "We built our lives according to deep intimacies that are dear and precious to us. We don't want to be forced by laws or statutes to cross into those intimate things where we don't want to go."

He suggested strongly that black people did not possess the same kind of soul before God that white people owned, attacking the "spurious doctrine" of national church groups preaching the "universal Fatherhood of God and brotherhood of man." He suggested that the best thing white people could do for black people was force isolation on them: "It is a kindness and goodness to them that they go to a colored church, while we seek to develop our own people in our own church."

He summoned images of integrationists as dirty, foreign, loathsome beings, Godless people who occupied a place somewhere in the direction of "up there."

"Any man who says he is altogether integrated is soft in the head. Let them integrate. Let them sit up there in their dirty shirts and make all their fine speeches. But they're all a bunch of infidels, dying from the neck up."

Leaders at home were concerned because Criswell was speaking directly and specifically against court-ordered desegregation, suggesting that, even though desegregation was now the law of the land, those who espoused obeying that law were bad citizens and bad churchmen: "Desegregating where we live is the stirring up of our people over a cause that, as of now, is not wisely presented. The people who seek to further this among us are not in sympathy with the great spiritual aims of our churches."

When they had gathered their breath and composed themselves after Criswell's speech, the response from the national Baptist leadership was mainly negative. Billy Graham said that he had never agreed with Criswell on race, that his own views were well known, and he declined to comment beyond that. Dr. Stewart A. Norman of the Southeastern Baptist Seminary at Wake Forest rose from the assemblage at Columbia and said, "It is a sorry day in the history of Baptists when we damn those who choose to differ with us.

"The voice with which we speak today," Norman said, meaning Criswell's voice, "sounds more of weakness than of confident strength, as if, from fear and real uneasiness, we turn upon our fellow Christians with scathing criticisms."

Back home in Dallas, some white clergy spoke out against the

Criswell speech, an act of considerable courage at the time. Dr. Harry Sarles of City Temple Presbyterian said, "I feel that the church should lead the way in implementing the Supreme Court decision on segregation. I cannot reconcile the Holy Scripture with any kind of discrimination."

The response from the black clergy was clear and direct. The Reverend Ernest C. Estell, pastor of St. John's Baptist Church and the man who had spoken so strongly against the bombings in the early fifties, made it plain that nothing Criswell said was going to change anything.

". . . the Negro will achieve first class citizenship in this country in spite of all that is said and done to the contrary. And we want it known that we are going to employ every legitimate and peaceful means to that end."

Other black clergy were obviously shocked and hurt by Criswell's speech. I. B. Loud, pastor of St. Paul Methodist and a conservative leader who always urged accommodation with the whites, said, "Such views do not reflect the man I thought I knew. The church has a definite responsibility to promote and create good race relations, not create more chaos."

There were, however, influential white clergy in Dallas who agreed with Criswell, who took his side and seemed relieved that he had stepped into the breach for them. The Reverend Ralph H. Langley, pastor of Wilshire Baptist Church, said, "At the time, I am in agreement with the Supreme Court's decision that the Negro should have first-class citizenship rights. But I feel separate and equal facilities for the Negro satisfies this aim, and that it will be many, many years before this section of the country will be ready for complete integration."

16

For all the control the oligarchy seemed to have accomplished with the accommodation reached by the blue-ribbon grand jury, the signals to the citizenry of the city were growing increasingly mixed and confusing again. There were white people of conscience in the community who believed that desegregation was just and right; the business leadership, as usual, was already tilting toward accommodation, certainly in those areas where the law had already spoken. But there was genuine disarray building, too. Even the business leadership seemed intent on holding some things back, where there were special ritual considerations. And nothing was of greater ritual importance to the business leadership than the State Fair.

Since the 1930s, blacks had been admitted to the fair on a special day set aside just for them. On that one day, during the fair's run of several weeks, black schools were locked; black children were bused to the fairgrounds; and the State Fair of Texas entertained the blacks. Commonly and more or less openly called "Nigger Day" by white people through the 1940s, the day was redubbed "Negro Achievement Day" by fair officials in the early 1950s, fooling no one. Under increasing pressure to abolish Nigger Day and completely desegregate, the fair finally opened its gates to blacks during its entire run in 1953, but black people were still barred from the midway and the restaurants. They could go to the barns and admire the fine hogs people in the country had grown that season, but only on Negro Achievement Day were they allowed to enter the midway, buy cotton candy and throw beanbags into the mouths of plywood clowns.

Already by the mid-1950s, a divergence was beginning to be visible between black leaders in Dallas, who were cautious and conservative in the main, and black leaders in much of the rest of Texas, who were less patient. It fell to black leaders elsewhere in Texas, for example, to challenge the grudging pace of desegregation at the State Fair in Dallas. In 1955, the Brownwood Chapter of the NAACP attacked Negro Achievement Day, saying it was a barely dressed-up vestige of an abhorrent racist past in Texas. But Dallas black leaders defended the fair. John W. Rice, manager of the Dallas Negro Chamber of Commerce, said the fair "does not practice segregation in any manner." Rice, who had been put in charge of arrangements for black activities at the fair, said, "About 15,000 or 20,000 colored people already have attended the fair this year."

Not very much farther into the fair's run, however, black people complained to the Dallas Negro Chamber that the fair which the chamber claimed was desegregated was still very much segregated. Was the Dallas Negro Chamber of Commerce an agent of segregation? Even though the midway had been partially opened up, several of the rides and almost all of the eating places would still not serve blacks. The Negro Chamber, in deference to this irrefutable truth, suddenly withdrew its support of the fair.

The iron grip of the Dallas oligarchy over this supposedly statewide event was never more visible or important than during this time. Dallas Mayor R. L. Thornton offered to open up some more of the fair but said certain eating establishments and rides simply would have to remain separate. Two rides in particular were of special concern to Mayor Thornton and struck him and his fellow Dallas oligarchs on the Fair Board as being clearly beyond the reach of even the most radical assertions of right. They were "Laff in the Dark" and "Dodge 'Em Scooter." These two rides, it seemed, involved physical contact — the possible if not certain touching of black skin to white skin and, presumably, vice versa — which was, in Mayor Thornton's view, an obvious impossibility. Somewhere in that opinion, the Supreme Court surely must have said, "none of the above applies, however, to 'Laff in the Dark' or 'Dodge 'Em Scooter.' "

In 1956, the Dallas Negro Chamber of Commerce finally and belatedly picked up the flag for the rest of the state's black population and told the white Dallas business leaders that they wanted "Laff in the Dark" and "Dodge 'Em Scooter," the restaurants, the whole ball of wax, everything the white people had, or they would not reinstate their support of the fair. Thornton refused to move.

He called the chamber's action "regrettable" and suggested that the fair had far more important things to offer blacks than rides and restaurants. Gone were all the blue lagoons and skyrockets Thornton invoked when commending the fair to white people. Instead, for blacks, there were good solid, uplifting qualities of the fair from which they were absenting themselves needlessly. He insisted that the fair was not segregated, and he said: "The State Fair of Texas has worked diligently, for this long period of years, has had for its objective the improvement of agriculture, livestock, scientific invention, amusement, entertainment — all for the benefit of all races and creeds — and it is indeed regrettable that, in a great city and a great country like this, the Dallas Negro Chamber of Commerce sees fit to withdraw its support from an institution that has done so much for this city and for the people of all races in this southwestern country."

Thornton's word was final, and it was law. The fair continued to be a bastion of formal institutional racism long after Thornton's role had ended. In the mid-1960s, a decade after the battle to keep "Laff in the Dark" racially pure, the State Fair of Texas would still be deciding which child in Texas that year had raised the best Negro pig or chicken and which had been the best New Negro Homemaker or New Negro Farmer of the Year.

The State Fair has always been a focus of murmurs and undercurrents that go on to become major themes in the culture of the city, as it was in demonstrating the eagerness of the Negro Chamber to accommodate Thornton as long as possible, thereby cutting the black leadership of Dallas away from black sentiment elsewhere in Texas for a while. In Thornton's assertion in 1956 that the fair simply was not segregated, even though people of different races would not be allowed to mingle together in "Laff in the Dark," there was the beginning of another Dallas tradition that endures to this day — the willingness of white people in Dallas to assert that, in this once rigidly segregated and still dramatically separated city, racial separation does not exist and never has existed. This is a remarkable notion, impossible to take seriously were it not offered so often and so confidently.

What exists, by this view, is simple good sense: not letting people whose forebears came from Donegal get into "Dodge 'Em Scooter" with people whose forebears came from Basutoland isn't segregation.

It's common sense. Segregation is when you separate blacks and whites for silly or illogical reasons, and nothing that is done in Dallas is ever silly or illogical.

In 1961, when the Metropolitan Opera announced it no longer could appear at facilities on the fairgrounds in Dallas because of racially segregated seating in the Music Hall there, John Rosenfield, a popular music critic in Dallas, blamed the decision on pressure from the NAACP and said that everyone in Dallas knew the Music Hall on the fairgrounds was not segregated.

He suggested that blacks had to sit in the back of the auditorium because they had been such poor supporters of the arts in the past. "Negro interest in high-priced events never has been rampant." If they wanted to sit up front with the white folks, they needed to subscribe, to kick in, but Rosenfield doubted that any of that was their intent at all:

"If the interests of the cultured Negro, for example, are genuine to the extent of wanting to hear the best opera from a very good seat, one could tell him how to go about it. If it is a new idea, inspired more to 'test' segregation than to patronize the arts, he may meet with a certain amount of frustration that has nothing to do with his race."

In a final dismissal borrowed directly from the philosophical tradition of the State Fair of Texas and the entrenched business priesthood of the city, Rosenfield demanded of his hypothetical black American: "Where was he when civic leaders were scrounging for financial guarantees in the effort to develop the city?"

"He," of course, was probably scrounging for food and shelter, scrounging to get through high school, to avoid starvation and typhus in West Dallas, to go to college and hope one day to hear some good opera. But, already in Dallas, there was only one "there," one place and time that conferred legitimacy — having been there when the State Fair was born, and having been white at the time.

17

Once Brown v. The Board of Education was on the table, it was clear to the oligarchy that Dallas would have to accommodate the law somehow. Torn as they may have been over the State Fair, the reservoir-and-levee gang knew that keeping the peace was the only way to keep the business ball rolling, and keeping the business ball rolling was the only thing that counted. That was why Criswell's demagoguery on the race issue posed such a threat. But Criswell could be dealt with. He may have been independent, but he wasn't that independent. There was by then an even greater threat to civic peace in the city.

A simple, cruel, ironic political equation was at work in Dallas at the time, but, like the overall dynamic of the black struggle, this equation was too close at hand for the leadership to read. For every ounce of effort the leadership invested in preserving the peace of the city through authoritarian control, Dallas became that much more a hotbed of absolutist extremism. It all operated according to forces that the leadership itself had set in motion when it began pulling the city in on itself and relieving the citizenry of the day-to-day drudgery of government and politics.

Severed from ordinary local politics in America, cut off from the processes by which people in other cities got streetlights fixed and streets repaired, rank-and-file Dallasites floated free in a kind of political slip-zone. They may have voted for state officials, and they talked about voting for presidents and senators. They did take some close interest in United States representatives from time to time. But in most cities, in the ordinary scheme of things, in places where populations are diverse and conflicts are complex, the surface where Americans establish touch with the American democracy, where they make real contact and feel the system's skin, is in local politics. Grand national themes are fine, principle is fine, but you never know how things really work until you go downtown and try to get your neighbor cited for uncut weeds. Then the next time someone says, "We should teach Castro a lesson," you may think to yourself, "Great, I just hope it's easier than teaching my neighbor a lesson."

Ordinary Dallasites weren't allowed to think about weeds. They were only supposed to think of Dallas as a whole. And they weren't even supposed to think about the whole out loud unless they were on the right guest lists. The political soul of the rank and file began to float, to turn free and tumble without fixed axis.

There it all was. On the front page, next to the picture of Governor Shivers calling for a vote on interposition, was the picture of a former lawyer for the National Labor Relations Board, a probable commie, snapping her saucy briefcase shut during a recess of the House Un-American Activities Committee. Side by side, right on the front page, and it all made perfect sense, ultimate sense, extreme sense if you weren't particularly tacked down anyway. What was scourge enough in the rest of the country would become physical passion in Dallas. McCarthyism worked a miracle in Dallas. Eventually, the force of ideas would deal a vicious blow and a surprise to the men who had believed with all their hearts and souls that dirt and bricks were where real power dwelled.

In February 1956, on the very day Criswell was delivering the speech in favor of racial and religious segregation in South Carolina, a body called the Dallas County Patriotic Council appeared before the Dallas Park Board and demanded to know who was responsible for the "large proportion of works by communist artists displayed in the Dallas Museum of Fine Arts." The meeting between the group and the board had begun in the offices of Park Director L. B. Houston but boiled over quickly into the auditorium in the Public Library, where members of the park board were subjected to a series of diatribes on the dangers of communist art.

Bill Ware, a vice commander of the American Legion Metropolitan Post, said it was obvious that the presence of communist art in the museum had been "caused by someone." It had been, he said, "planned and motivated. In our museum, someone has to be motivating this thing."

Reading from a pamphlet the group had prepared for the occasion, Colonel Alvin Owsley, former ambassador to Ireland and past president of the American Legion, narrowed things down, "The arbitrary and uncompromising attitude of certain members of the board of trustees of the Dallas Art Museum have taken and widely publicized, reaffirming their expressed will and intention to exhibit the works of art of communists, communist fronters or fellow travelers — the Reds — has done the museum vast and irreparable harm and lessened its future usefulness in our community."

Owsley warned the board that the city's taxpayers would probably stop supporting the museum if it continued to show "red art," and then he explained how red art worked its wiles: "It is one of the basic premises of Communist doctrine that art can and should be used in the constant process of attempting to brainwash and create public attitudes that are soft toward communism."

Because the museum and museum board were hierarchically subservient to the park board, Ware said the Patriotic Council wanted the park board to adopt a formal policy rejecting any and all art from the city-owned museum that had been created by "artists known to be identified with subversive activities."

"We urge that in the future artists clearly identified with subversive activities in this country have their works banned from exhibition."

Finally, after an hour and a half of bizarre harangues and broad innuendo about certain members of the art museum board, the meeting ended. Park Board Chairman Ray Hubbard promised the assemblage he would give their proposal serious thought, and he meant it. The museum trustees had been battling with the issue for almost a year and had even, at one point, adopted a policy against acquiring any additional "red art," apparently agreeing that they already had an adequate supply. That policy was overturned, and in the end the museum was allowed to show anybody's art it wanted except the work of Pablo Picasso, who, after all, had said right out that he was one. But, at the height of the flap and before it was settled, the city took the Bill Wares and Colonel Owsleys of its midst quite seriously.

What if there really was communist art on the walls of the museum after all, something somebody had slipped in there somehow without anyone realizing it? What effect would it have on people to look at it? Indeed, why did certain parties allow communist art to get into the museum? Everyone knew at whom the innuendoes were aimed. The most important target on the board of the museum did happen to be a Democrat, a liberal Democrat at that, and he did not happen to be a Christian. Maybe it might not be a bad idea to call this certain party on the carpet, the one suspected of being subversive, and see what he had to say for himself.

So Stanley Marcus was called to account for himself. Seen now by the world outside Dallas as a merchandising genius, Marcus is today within Dallas an elder statesman, survivor of battles and bearer of many scars. He did more than survive the period of the 1950s and early 1960s when they were painting swastikas on Jewish-owned stores in Dallas. He emerged with more than personal vindication. His view of life and morality, in the end, took deeper root and did more to feed the nature of the new city than the views of any of his interrogators in the 1950s.

Marcus surveys Dallas now from the top of the Republic Bank Tower, where he occupies a suite of offices provided him by Carter-Hawley-Hale, the people who bought his family's store. He is attended by a loyal cadre of middle-aged women who, in all personal references to their employer, use the distinctly honorific "Mr. Stanley." There is consternation if Mr. Stanley's request for a diet cola is handled inefficiently. But for an elder statesman and especially for a Dallas statesman of any age, Marcus is informal and warm with visitors. The hard edge still shows, of course, when he talks about communist art. He was chairman of the museum board at the time.

"We had taken on a show being sponsored by Sports Illustrated, called "Sports in Art," to benefit the Olympic teams going to Australia. I got a call from Fred Florence, who was president of Republic Bank. He said, 'You better get over here. I understand you've got a lot of communist art works coming to the museum.' "

Marcus hurried over to Florence's office, but, once there, Marcus asked the salient question. "I said, 'What is a communist work of art?'

"He said, 'Well this one, Number 13.' It was by Ben Shahn. It was called 'The National Pastime' and it was a picture of a man hitting a baseball. I said, 'I don't know how anybody could think hitting a baseball was communist.' Another one was of a man catching a fish. I said, 'Well, I don't think too many people think fishing is communist, either.' "

Florence told Marcus that the foes of "red art" had threatened to picket the Neiman-Marcus store, which was cosponsoring the show, if the museum didn't cancel. "I said, 'As far as I'm concerned, you can tell them I said go to hell, and as far as the museum is concerned, we can't cancel the show.'"

Knowing the matter was not closed until the main players in the oligarchy had been won over, Marcus hit the campaign trail immediately. The five pictures singled out on Florence's list as being definitely communist were Shahn's baseball picture, "Fisherman" by William Zorach, "The Park" and "Winter" by Leon Kroll, and "Skaters" by Yasuo Kuniyoshi. Marcus immediately set about consulting Dallas leaders to see which ones believed the public should be informed that, in Dallas at that time, it was now considered subversive to play baseball, skate, fish, go to the park or throw snowballs.

That evening he cornered Ted Dealey, president of the Dallas Morning News, at his home. "I asked him if he believed in freedom of speech. He said, 'Sure.' I asked him if he believed in freedom of expression. He said, 'Of course.' I told him if he believed in those things, he'd better believe in freedom of art. Then I went to see Tom Gooch at the Times Herald, and I told him about Owsley. He said, 'Tell the old fart to come around me, and we'll blow his torpedoes.'"

One after another, Marcus rolled them up until he was assured of victory. "The Sports in Art" controversy was only one of several flares over "red art" in Dallas in that period. Red scares were not unique to Dallas, but the intensity and wild invention of the "red art" paranoia was a uniquely Dallas phenomenon. The "Sports" show had already appeared at the Boston Museum of Fine Arts and the Corcoran Gallery in Washington, and it had not occurred to anyone in those places to see treachery in the paintings themselves.

For a long time after Marcus had won the battle over "red art," the Dallas museum was still loathe to acquire or hang any contemporary art. "They associated contemporary art with everything that was Godless," Marcus said.

Marcus, always acting as one of the city's tethers to the beyond, organized a special show called "Some American Businessmen Collect Contemporary Art." This time, when he hit the campaign trail, Marcus pulled strings in the outside world, calling on people in whose presence he knew many of the city's business leaders would be humbled. Smiling, he said, "People in a city the size of Dallas always have respect for someone in a bigger city.

"I called David Rockefeller and asked him for a picture for the show, and then I asked him to tell any banking associates he might have in Dallas that he had lent a picture for this show and he wanted them to go make sure it was properly hung."

On through the ranks of business and the professions he marched, calling on this national figure and that to chip in a picture, always making it plain that he wanted more than the picture: He wanted a crowd of very attentive, very respectful Dallas bigshots down there oohing and ahhing over all the contemporary art their associates, heros, bankers, note-holders and permission-givers in other cities had collected.

18

At the time of the communist art controversy, the oligarchy had grown uncharacteristically unsure of its footing. The Dallas way of doing things required that the city find some way to accommodate the new court decisions on desegregation and avoid riots at all costs. But the disparate and divisive forces the oligarchy had been able to quell in the matter of the bombings seemed to be welling up again in the city, and it wasn't clear precisely where in this new problem the oligarchy itself should stand. On the one hand, the Colonel Owsleys and Bill Wares of the world found more than a little sympathy for their views among the main body of the city's arch-conservative elite. On the other hand, they meant trouble, and there was enough of that gathering without them.

The establishment's memory of this long and troubled prologue to desegregation is predictably neat and self-serving, a version of history that went public with the publication in 1964 of Warren Leslie's book, *Dallas, Public and Private*. The official version is this: Being of typically pragmatic and business-like mind, the establishment shrugged, decided to make the best of a bad deal and set about orchestrating one of the smoothest desegregations of public institutions and activities in the nation's history.

If there is any quantity of truth in this tale, it may be the part in which, after agony and great travail, business interest wins out in the end. Otherwise, this story, so easily and generally accepted in the white community of Dallas today as to be on a par with Washington's cherry tree and Davey Crockett's last stand, is incomplete in a degree that verges on the fantastic. Not surprisingly, what it keeps entirely from view is the role black people played in pushing the oligarchy out of its moral and philosophical muddle and into compliance with the law. It ignores the fact that, when Dallas finally did submit to token desegregation of its public schools, it did so nearly a half decade after Little Rock and only then with political guns trained on it from inside and out. It's certainly understandable that business leaders in Dallas would propagate this story and, like the one about the fair not being segregated, eventually would talk themselves into believing it.

Without a good deal of hard pushing, in point of fact, the oligarchy was not headed anywhere in a hurry. Since early 1954, the Dallas Morning News had been coaching the white community bluntly on what it and the levee boys obviously thought should be the new white strategy, which was to go along with legal desegregation, obey the letter of the law, wait, be calm, do nothing that would disturb commerce or the peace of the city, and then find new and informal ways to maintain actual and total separation of the races. The Dallas Morning News even suggested that the courts had probably envisioned such a response and would do nothing to countervene it, paralleling earlier local optimism about the inevitability of a return to slavery:

"Southern people who do not believe in integration should work out a retreat from legal separation by as common sense a procedure as possible," the Morning News said on its editorial page.

"The Supreme Court specifically provided for at least a start in this direction.

"After all, 'segregation' of races throughout the world is largely individual choice, not by law . . . .

"The court ruling for abandonment of legal separation has shocked southern whites, yet its implications are not nearly as great as might appear on the surface.

"Actually the decision stands or falls on acceptance by the public. If the people of the United States want to integrate at the local level, the court's opinion will survive. If they do not, there will be circumvention, and the probability is that the court will close its eyes."

Again, black leaders had to step forward and warn Dallas there would be no dispensation, that black people in Dallas wanted every single thing the court ruling promised. In September 1955, the NAACP made certain that black students in Dallas would show up at white schools to register for the term. Almost 30 black students were turned away, and the NAACP immediately took the school district to court.

Dr. B. E. Howell, chairman of the Dallas NAACP executive committee, was constrained to deliver the message again to Dallas: "The parents of school-age Negroes in Dallas want their children to receive the best possible training under the most favorable learning conditions. They want their children treated fairly and justly as all other children are treated.

"They resent the arbitrary 'go-slow' attitude of the board of education."

Another aspect in which Leslie's historical account of desegregation in Dallas diverges from truth is in the monolithic nature that it posits for the oligarchy at the time. In fact, as this enormous and ferocious issue moved through time and the city, it parted the oligarchy in telling ways. At the same time the NAACP was working to make sure Dallas remembered it was still a part of the external world, people like Stanley Marcus were working from within to convince the oligarchy that they had but one choice: Make it work. Really work.

"As it turned out," Marcus says now, "the people of Dallas were way ahead of their leaders, as they usually are." In spite of the cynicism of the News' suggestion that people hold out and wait for it all to go away, there were strong indications that the oligarchy might have been giving the white people of Dallas short shrift, that the people of Dallas might be able to live with desegregation more peacefully than their betters had been willing to imagine. Working through a night in April 1956, Dallas Transit System workers pulled down the hated signs — 12 in each bus, including one white porcelain sign quoting the segregation laws of the State of Texas — and sent desegregated buses out onto the streets of Dallas the next morning to gather riders. While the Citizens Council held its breath, the people of Dallas climbed aboard the buses as they always had, and rode to work, as they always had.

That morning, W. R. Burns, president of the bus company, said, "We are merely doing what every legitimate American organization must do — complying with the decision of the nation's highest tribunal."

Later in the day, a Dallas Transit System dispatcher said, "People are riding just as they always have." At the end of a problem-free day, Burns issued a statement: "We are immensely gratified by the law-abiding manner in which the people of Dallas have accepted the U.S.

Supreme Court's decision where municipal buses are concerned."

The Dallas Morning News' suggestion that it couldn't work had been proven wrong. In fact, it could work. It did work. It worked because people had to get to work. If the buses were the only way to get from here to there, and if the buses weren't segregated, then people had to climb up on the buses and get used to it. For all the free-floating zaniness that seemed to have infected the air in the fifties, for all the communist art controversies and for all the dark memories of the outbreaks in South Dallas just a few years earlier, the white rank and file of the city nevertheless had shown itself to be possessed of a reasonable core, of an ability to shrug and go about its business. Dallas didn't have to disobey the law. Dallas didn't have to be violent.

It was to this reasonable center, with its immense respect for law, order, and good citizenship, that the Stanley Marcuses of the city would urge the oligarchy to appeal. After all, the courts had spoken: It wasn't going to go away no matter what the Dallas Morning News or anyone else said. Why not get through it as smoothly as possible, with as few bruises to the structure as possible? Why not do it the way Little Rock had wanted to but failed to pull off? It was time for the business leadership to get off dead center and start leading, before someone else did.

19

The heartening performance of white people in desegregation of the city's buses did not by any stretch of the imagination mean the voices of division in the city had been quelled. On the contrary, they were gaining strength as the moment of truth approached. With Bible in hand, the Reverend Earl Anderson, 63-year-old pastor of the Munger Place Baptist Church, was calling for 20,000 white people in Dallas, "openly committed to the principle of purity of the races," to help in the fight being waged by the Texas' Citizens Council for segregation.

In tones and terms being heard all too frequently around the city, Anderson said, "Negroes who understand God's teachings don't want to mix with us . . . they have as much right to a pure race as we do.

"Negroes believe mixing races is disobedient to the word of God."

In the late 1950s and early 1960s, few people in the white American mainstream were terribly sure just what was meant by the phrase, token desegregation. When black people told them token desegregation was the admission of only a few black persons into all-white institutions for purely ceremonial purposes, most white people blinked and thought to themselves, "But I thought that *was* desegregation." In Dallas, even the ritual introduction of a single black student into the midst of white students was deeply feared, especially if that black student were a boy, because of the dread of sexual intimacy between the races and of interracial marriage, then called "amalgamation."

The difference between desegregation and tokenism had to be explained for whites in Dallas by Clarence Laws, Southwest regional director of the NAACP, and Laws had to go to New York and give a speech at Fordham University to do it. The white newspapers in Dallas had taken little note of what Laws had to say when he was in town, but they took careful note of his speech in New York in May 1961. Laws explained that tokenism allowed "segregationists to concentrate all their hate and violence at one point and upon a few hapless children and their parents."

He went on to say that the rules Dallas had dreamed up to frustrate any attempts at true segregation of the schools were "the most rigid to be found anywhere." He said that real desegregation in Dallas would not be accomplished unless the people of Dallas met two conditions, "First, responsible citizens must show sufficient concern about the rights of Negroes and the good name of the city, and second, the school board must not repeat the desegregation farce that was witnessed at Little Rock and New Orleans."

The white business leadership, by then, was in partial agreement with Laws. The leaders, too, had decided that the city would need to summon all of its respect for black rights, all of its concern for the good name of the city, and every ounce of its organizational and motivational ability for what lay ahead. The difference was that the white leaders believed all of those things were necessary in order to accomplish the most meager tokenism attainable, to avoid riots in the short term and, in the longer run, to stave off the horrors of miscegenation. No one had any intention of doing anything beyond that, certainly not in the schools, certainly not in the neighborhoods.

The background against which the school decision played was one rising tension on the homefront. In the late 1950s and early 1960s, white Dallas developers were still building Negro subdivisions, modeled on the great success at Hamilton Park. The builders expected and quite often received the earnest thanks of the Dallas black middle class for their efforts. In 1959, when James Smith was developing the Highland Hills subdivision near Bishop College on Simpson-Stuart Road in far South Dallas, he acknowledged that a few black people had objected to the creation of a deliberately all-black neighborhood, but he said they were definitely in the minority. Smith said most black people frankly preferred to live in all-black areas.

There was some truth in what Smith said. Middle-class black people in Dallas by now were noticeably confused about which they preferred — to live wherever they pleased, or to live where their families would be safe. One reason why some black families might still have preferred life in racial enclaves in Dallas was that, by 1960, white intimidation of blacks moving into white neighborhoods had started up again, this time in the Oak Cliff section of town, high on the bluffs over the Trinity River.

Oak Cliff, on what everyone has always agreed is the most attractive terrain in the otherwise unrelievedly flat Dallas landscape, happened to be the white middle-class area closest to black middle-class neighborhoods, in a natural and gradual line of migration for upwardly mobile blacks. But white Oak Cliff residents were already developing what was to become a long tradition of paranoia based on the belief that North Dallas was causing black people to come to Oak Cliff by racial steering practices in the real estate business.

Oak Cliff also happened to have remained a fairly cohesive enclave of native white Texans, with a strong community identity, distinct and separate from the new Sunbelt mix of Yankees and other foreigners already beginning to congregate across the river and in North Dallas. Ironically, this very feeling of deeply rooted neighborhood loyalty and distinctness from the rest of Dallas, along with the level of ethnic mixture at which Oak Cliff finally settled, has made Oak Cliff all the more attractive in recent years to incoming Yankees seeking relief from the barrenness of the new suburbs north of town.

But when black families began moving into white Oak Cliff in the late fifties and early sixties, it began to look as if the same problems associated with the bombings in South Dallas a few years earlier might materialize again, a prospect that worried the Citizens Council and that was only getting worse as white people in Oak Cliff began to feel more and more as if they were being steered into a confrontation. Things started off slowly, as they had in the past, with expressions of "concern" by "reasonable members of the community" and spokesmen for neighborhood groups and "associations."

The Reverend P. L. Young, a black minister who made the mistake of buying a house in the Shannon Estates area, an all-white enclave on Linnet Lane, was still trying to load the boxes into his new home when white people started appearing on his lawn and ringing the phone. Finally the crowd on his lawn had grown to sufficient size that Reverend Young felt compelled to call the police. Everyone was still being very polite when the police arrived, speaking in controlled tones, explaining to Young that he had made some kind of mistake, but, after a while, even the police grew concerned about the situation. One officer told the crowd, "It just isn't good citizenship to stand around like this." One of the white neighbors who was not standing on the minister's lawn had another word for it. Watching from afar, he called what his neighbors were doing "gestapo tactics."

"I don't want to live with Negroes. But they have a right to buy houses here if they want to. They're living on the street behind us now and in the blocks adjacent to us. The association people are trying to keep anyone from buying or selling."

Before this scene of quiet ferocity had ended, Reverend Young had agreed to give up the home he had just purchased for his family. "I didn't know there was any resentment," he said, "or I wouldn't have tried to move. All I want is my money back and to live where I'm wanted."

The next day, Young went to some lengths to make it clear that he would depart quietly and without rancor. "I was advised to talk to the U.S. Attorney, but I'm not going to talk to anybody. I just want to sell that house and live where I'm wanted. I'm not affiliated with any pressure group. I'm not an agitator. The people asked me not to move in, and I obeyed them."

The apparent passivity of the Dallas black middle class had become a cause for concern among black leaders from other parts of the country who visited Dallas in 1960. Roy Wilkins of the NAACP put his prepared speech aside during a major address to the Dallas black community at Dallas Memorial Auditorium and lashed out against "the spineless attitude of some Negroes who are afraid to stand up and be counted on the side of freedom."

In this instance, Wilkins certainly could not have been accused of preaching to the choir. The entire choir, in fact, had failed to show up, because some of the members were school district employees. All black school district employees in Dallas had been given the distinct impression that they would lose their jobs if school superintendent W. T. White found out they had even listened to a speech about the NAACP, let alone taken part in one of its affairs.

On another occasion, Zan Holmes, a sophisticated, scholarly but tough young Methodist minister in Hamilton Park, moved from other themes in his sermon to a discussion of the NAACP. He was interrupted and informed that everyone in the church who worked for the school district would have to leave if he continued to discuss the NAACP.

Roy Wilkins had run into this kind of intimidation all over the South, and he wasn't buying it. Black people elsewhere were standing up to that kind of bully boy stuff, and it angered him that more black people in Dallas were not doing the same. "I understand that some school teachers were in the choir. They were afraid of criticism, or that they might lose their jobs if they came to sing for the NAACP.

"They ought to know they can't be free until they think they are free."

He told the Dallas audience a strange and exciting secret — that not only were there white people elsewhere in the world who worked with and for the NAACP, but that there were such white people in Dallas, Texas. "White people helped organize the NAACP. White people are helping us every day right here in Dallas."

Wilkins spoke of another phenomenon of which black people in Dallas had heard only whispers — the lunch counter sit-ins. Within weeks, black people would begin to break the color line in restaurants and bus stations all over the South. There would be arrests and headlines in Orangeburg, South Carolina; Atlanta, Georgia; and ultimately, unbelievably, in Dallas, Texas. Wilkins tried to put a bluff face on it. "We get hungry, just like anybody else." But none of his audience saw even the faintest humor in what seemed to them to be an appallingly dangerous enterprise.

20

wo months after Wilkins had chastised blacks in Dallas for their hesitance, Ashton Jones, a black minister from California, broke the line at three Dallas lunch counters. Dallas blacks only stared in disbelief. "I wish some of the Negroes who stood and watched us go in had followed," Reverend Jones said. Jones' entreaty would not go unheeded forever. The pressure from without would feed the pressure from within, no matter how conservative some of the leaders of the black community had become. But, for the moment, black people in Dallas were hanging far back.

The other side, meanwhile, certainly was not hanging back. The group defeated by Marcus over the "red art" exhibition affair, far from feeling vanquished, was back at work as never before, joining forces with the White Citizens Council (no relation to the Citizens Council) in demanding special anticommunism courses in all the public schools. Clarence Laws made certain the NAACP was represented at their meetings with the school board. "The communists would like nothing more than to see us divided .... Our strength lies in our unity, not our division," Laws told the board.

No one could fault that reasoning in public. But, of course, none of the white communism fighters were buying it in private. By then, anticommunism in Dallas had become almost equal with racism — part of a growing movement of extremism and intolerance, opposed to everything from Marx to modern art. The extremists, the racists and the wingdings in Dallas were no longer describable as a fringe group. There were enough of them around, after all, to send Bruce Alger to Washington.

Congressman Alger specialized in a kind of potpourri of outrageous, intolerant, and apocalyptic views in which he occasionally hit on fragments of truth in spite of himself. "If race riots come," Alger said, "and God forbid that should happen, they will be in the Northern racial tinder-box areas where reside our liberal friends urging this legislation."

The other half of this equation was that, no matter what the cause, no matter what the cost, Dallas was already making up its mind that there would be no riot in Dallas. Already in 1960, City Councilman Joe Geary wanted to know whether Dallas was ready, and the answer was that Dallas was very ready. Police Chief Carl F. Hansson, the man who had taken so much time to catch the white bombers a decade earlier, was wasting no time whatever in getting ready for rioters.

The usage at the time is of great significance. The word, riot, meant black people. The people who had done most of the rioting so far were white, but in 1960, everywhere in America, when white people used the term, riot, they meant what black people do when they run wild.

Hansson told the city council that Dallas had done what communities all over America were doing in 1960: It had purchased specially outfitted stationwagons, scientifically designed by law enforcement experts for the quelling of riots, along with special riot spotlights, antiriot loudspeakers, riot-stopping tear gas, special antiriot ropes and other equipment, all purchased by Chief Hansson after a visit to Little Rock, where police officials were recouping some of their lost prestige at the time by serving as consultants on what a riot is like. A special manual had been prepared and a riot-control course was being taught at the Oak Cliff substation, in which officers were reminded that, "regardless of your private views regarding minority groups, you, as officers of the law, must not compromise the performance of your public duty."

Far from treating the concept of tokenism as any sort of pejorative, the police course promised that it would be the official policy of the community. Officers were reassured that integration would not be "mass," because "most Negroes prefer to be with members of their own race and prefer to attend Negro schools, if this can be accomplished without undue hardship."

While black people in Dallas may have been ducking NAACP meetings and sit-ins downtown, out in the neighborhoods where they had to live there was less and less room to hide. White arson of black homes had begun again. The terror was building.

When it started for H. L. DeVaughn, it could have been the work of pranksters. Eggs were smashed against the walls of the new home just purchased in a white area by DeVaughn, who was baseball coach at the all-black Lincoln High School. Then rocks smashed through the windows. Then the bomb threats began.

"I'm hoping it's just a crank," DeVaughn said, trying to put the best face on it. Then he said, "Surely they know we have two small children living in the house."

As in the early 1950s, black people didn't put up with it forever without fighting back. Downtown, they were afraid to follow the minister from California into the white diners. Downtown, some were afraid to attend the NAACP rallies. But at home, where the wall was, where there was no more retreat, they were beginning to fight back. Mrs. H. L. Fagan, wife of a black insurance agent who had moved into a white enclave in east Oak Cliff four months earlier, woke her husband at 1 a.m. on the morning of July 21, 1960. She told him that she had just frightened off a gang of whites who were getting ready to light a wooden cross they had planted on the lawn.

Fagan grabbed his gun and raced out onto the lawn. The car full of whites was coming back around the block. As the car accelerated and sped by, Fagan pointed the gun at the passengers and fired, again and again. He had no idea if he had hit any of them. Black people in Dallas might not be willing to sit next to them at the lunch counter yet, but they sure would kill white people if all that Klan business was going to start up again in the neighborhoods.

New things were happening, within Dallas and in the world around it, too. Beginning in the mid-fifties and building as the decade passed, outsiders were deciding to stay away from Dallas specifically because it was so strictly segregated a city. Dallas had been especially stung in 1956, when a small contingent within the Veterans of Foreign Wars had tried to get a federal injunction barring the VFW's planned national encampment in Dallas that year. The effort was in vain, but in the years that followed, hoteliers and other convention-dependent business people in the city actually began complaining about the level of segregation, claiming it was losing the city lucrative convention business. In the same period, the people who had been put in charge

115

of recruiting new businesses to move to Dallas and fatten the Sunbelt boom were coming back with reports of Yankee companies that had declined, specifically citing racial segregation as a negative deciding factor. As if the prospect of losing business and money weren't bad enough, the federal appellate courts were growing more and more impatient with Dallas, openly criticizing the city at the end of the decade for dragging its feet in the matter of the schools.

Worse yet, by early 1961, the carefully machined racial peace on which the oligarchy prided itself was coming apart again, as it had threatened to do after the bombings in the early 1950s. The centerpiece of the arrangement, the biracial committee, now called the Committee of 14, was in distinct danger of becoming a committee of seven. The black members had been badly embarrassed in the black community by critics who said their continued membership on the committee was beginning to smack of treason in the face of ongoing formal segregation of the schools, the continued humiliation inflicted on blacks in stores downtown, and the galling treatment of blacks at the State Fair. The oligarchy, meanwhile, was not lifting a finger to bail out its trusted black friends on the committee. Mayor R. L. Thornton would not budge on the continued segregation of "Laff in the Dark" or of certain restaurants and other sacred corners of his beloved fairgrounds.

The accommodationist leadership of the black community found itself spread thin between the obdurate white oligarchy and an increasingly restive black community. In January of 1961, W. J. Durham, a lawyer and member of the Committee of 14, called for sit-ins and boycotts of the big downtown stores, Sanger's, Titche-Goettinger, H. L. Green and S. H. Kress & Company, and said that the Committee of 14 had broken apart. But, in an angry public denunciation of Durham that took Dallas' white and black leaders alike by surprise, H. Rhett James, pastor of the New Hope Baptist Church, leapt on Durham's call, saying it was hypocritical, suspect, and too little too late.

James said Durham and the other black members of the committee were only trying to save face after having been used by the white members to stave off any kind of effective black boycott or sit-in in Dallas. James was a leader in a whole new kind of black movement in Dallas, of a sort the oligarchy had not dealt with before. He didn't believe that accommodation led to action: He believed it worked the other way around. He and his followers had already been picketing the stores downtown for months, without so much as a nod from the black members of the biracial committee. He and his group had fanned the flames and built the heat that was building up again over the stores and the State Fair. He said the attempt of the old-style leaders from the biracial committee to get in on it and take over the demonstrations at this point came too late. Their past performance meant they couldn't be trusted to run things anyway.

"I had told the (black members of the) committee that action must precede negotiation," James said. "I told them that my group would not continue to go along under their illusion. Durham's statement was an opportunistic way of admitting that his group lacked virility all along. I led the picket line at H. L. Green's for nine weeks in November and December, the store's most vulnerable period, and I repeatedly sent wires after I stopped my demonstrations warning that they would be resumed again if the committee that Durham belongs to could get no action by January 14."

This was new. This was a black man who thought he had the right to argue from power. From force. Action preceding negotiation: This was the world turned upside down. Of course action preceded negotiation. White action. Eggs first, pranks in the night, and then, because that was never enough, rocks smashing through the windows, showering shards of glass on the children and the wives inside. Then the burning crosses: the savage heart of Christendom with blood in its eye. The bomb threats, and in the case of the really stubborn Negro interloper, the bomb itself, looping up slowly from the curb, dropping with a thump in the dirt next to the house, hissing red in the darkness. Exploding — sleep turned white, red and burning — terror that dripped down through the muscles and curled up sick in the pit of the stomach. And then there would be negotiations, because Dallas was a reasonable town and wanted no harm to come to any of its citizens if harm possibly could be avoided, harm and headlines being bad for commerce.

But this black man believed that he had a right to go downtown, throw up picket lines in front of white-owned stores and then demand negotiations on his terms. This was something entirely new welling up in the city.

21

In the spring of that same year, 1961, zig-zagging slowly across the South was a bus carrying seven black people and six white people, all members of the Congress of Racial Equality. They were being called "Freedom Riders," and their express purpose was to stir up the kind of "action" Rhett James was talking about, flouting the sacred traditions of segregation and urging others to do the same wherever they went.

The freedom riders were a moral knife, slicing into the very heart of Dixie. The deeper and the longer they rode, the more awful became the response. One was arrested in Charlotte, North Carolina. At the next stop, in Rock Hill, South Carolina, three were beaten. Two more were arrested in Winnsboro. A quiet stretch followed, and then the freedom riders struck out through upcountry Alabama and down into the black belt. There, six miles outside Anniston, Alabama, the Klan bombed one of the two buses they were riding, burned it, and were slowly and methodically beating the riders when the police arrived and fired guns in the air to stop them.

Then the horror grew even worse. In Birmingham, thugs armed with lengths of pipe beat the freedom riders for 30 minutes and put two in the hospital. The nation and the world watched, galvanized, unbelieving, filled with wrath and revulsion.

White officialdom in Dixie sympathized openly with the Klan and denounced the freedom riders as the worst sort of criminals. Alabama Governor John Patterson said: "I cannot guarantee protection for this bunch of rabble-rousers." Birmingham Police Chief Bull Connor said he had known ahead of time the attack in his city might occur but hadn't been able to send police officers: He said he had been short-handed because it was Mother's Day. Still, the freedom riders rode on, fully prepared to die.

More came. When a second group of freedom riders rolled into the bus terminal in Montgomery, Alabama, John Doar of the Civil Rights Division of the Justice Department was across the street in the U.S. Attorney's office with a phone jammed against his ear. On the other end was Attorney General Robert Kennedy and his deputy attorney general, Byron White. Kennedy and White heard Doar say: "The bus is in. The people are just standing there, watching .... Now the passengers are coming off. They're standing on a corner of the plat-form. Oh. There are fists. Punching! A bunch of men led by a guy with a bleeding face are beating them. There are no cops! It's terrible! It's terrible. There's not a cop in sight. People are yelling 'get 'em, get 'em.' It's awful. The cops are there now."

Montgomery Police Chief Lester B. Sullivan had refused to send in his men. The police who finally arrived were state troopers. Before it was over, the mob had broken one man's leg and had poured flam-mable liquid on another and ignited him. John Seigenthaler, Presi-dent Kennedy's personal envoy to deal with Montgomery officials, was dragged from his car, beaten and left unconscious in the street in a pool of his own blood for half an hour. All of Montgomery's white-owned ambulances reported they had suffered mechanical difficulties and could not answer calls to the scene.

It was in this context that the gentlemen of the Dallas Citizens Council decided to opt for moderation. By early 1961, the well-fought fight in the courts was at an end, and Dallas had been informed that it was subject to the same laws that ruled Little Rock and the rest of the country. It would have to desegregate. There would be no dispensa-tion. At that, the members of the Citizens Council were persuaded to their own decision to cooperate by a very specific wing of the Dallas business establishment — the wing that had always served as the city's foot in the real world, the half of the municipal personality that the rest of Texas least understood or trusted.

They were the merchants, the money men and the brokers. Without them, none of the levee gang's plans were going to go anywhere anyway. After all, the developer wing, dominated by good Scotch-Irish country folk and descendants of Confederate heroes, really were only building houses and office towers, warehouses and highways to service the new business created by the other wing, the people who were transforming Dallas into the financial and wholesaling center of the Southwest. It was the merchants and brokers, many of them from elsewhere originally, some of them even faintly liberal, all of them well traveled and educated, who really were in charge of the goose that laid the golden egg. The developers were in charge of the henhouse.

It is at this point that the version of things recounted ever since by the oligarchy begins to have some relationship with fact. Once the decision had been made, the Citizens Council was able to execute it with an authority and finality that could be summoned in no other part of the country, perhaps in few of the world's democracies, for that matter. Authority, after all, was Dallas's most abundant and respected political commodity.

Authority finally ruled the day. The desegregation of Dallas was ordered. It was to be instant. Total. Of course it would not entail real desegregation of the schools, the actual mixing of large numbers of children. That was never to occur. That still has not occurred. Nor would the neighborhoods integrate. The white neighborhoods, the better off ones anyway, could take care of themselves. As long as black people in Dallas stayed poor enough, there would be no great danger there. But the ceremonial desegregation of the city was to be complete and instant.

The banks called up every store, and every store called up every vendor, and the vendors told their suppliers, and the suppliers told their spouses who told their children. Stanley Marcus remembers it well:

"We had decided that Dallas would avoid a riot at all cost. The only course we could follow was to obey the law. We had a moral obligation on the part of the adults and the leadership to integrate all of the eating places and the toilets."

The eating places and the toilets. That may look trivial now, but it was to these very personal and physical settings that all of the deepest and strangest of the physical racial loathings of white people had been assigned.

22

Because the white establishment, and especially the Dallas Citizens Council types today, are so ready with the tale of Dallas' smooth and voluntary school desegregation in 1961, it's worth remembering, for the sake of history, that the Citizens Council acceded only at the last legal moment and only after its handpicked occupants of the local federal bench had been slapped down, reversed, and mortified by the appellate courts. During the years after the blowup at Little Rock, as the federal district judges in Dallas reached under every rock and into every corner of the law in search of a dispensation for Dallas, the appellate courts grew more and more impatient with the Dallas bench, citing its apparent disregard for, and ignorance of, the law and tradition. Even at that, in spite of the excoriating reversals and admonitions the Dallas bench had received already, United States District Judge T. Whitfield Davidson Jr. could not resist one last ill-fated stab at resistance.

In the summer of 1960, Judge Davidson tried to float a "voluntary" desegregation plan, which he more or less admitted wouldn't work, and he went on in his published opinion to explain why desegregation itself would never and should never work. The opinion is one of the last public statements of the white racist theory of race relations, reaching back directly into slavery and the unresolved injuries of Reconstruction and building into a crescendo of physical loathing as the judge enters the matter of interracial sex. His language is still powerful and significant: The fact that a federal district judge writing in 1960 spoke in a moral vocabulary still brutally crippled by the perversions of slave culture, still festered, unhealed by time — the fact that this generation of leadership has by no means passed from the scene in Dallas — says much about the role that slavery and its aftermath continue to play in white morality today.

In a long and rambling diatribe, Judge Davidson gets first to the moral question. He begins his discussion of slavery by reminding us there was never anything especially wrong with it since "it was the last fragment of an institution handed down to us from a universal practice and since everybody had been guilty, it was tolerated since the other fellow was doing it too." He leaps quickly from these transcendental questions to the practical matter of how very happy those black people must have been to be released from the terrible slave ships that had brought them (which they themselves had made quite a mess of by not having tidy personal habits) and finding themselves in the United States.

"A wild people from the desert, from the jungles on board a ship. They could not understand the language of the shipmaster. They knew not the use of sewerage even if any had been available. The very odor of the cargo was stifling to any that came near . . . .

"The Arab slave trader often brought him to a port . . . . No one knew his name, and it was yet some generations before he had a family or a surname. To be freed from his recent captors and from the foul condition of the ship was for a moment a relief, no doubt, to this poor fellow when he was inducted into the wide open space of a Southern plantation with open air, food, and kindness."

Judge Davidson tells us how one of the very first things the planter did, upon receiving a wild slave, was to teach him a few words of vocabulary and then begin immediately to teach him about the devil and especially about Hell, perhaps accounting for the frequency with which former slaves interviewed in this century mentioned Hell as the place where they supposed their former masters had gone. Then Davidson leads us through the fanciful version of the Civil War years that J. B. Cranfill had recounted for Dallas newspaper readers in 1941 — an obviously well-rehearsed and frequently retold myth of white slave culture, in which religion serves to keep the black man enslaved more effectively than chains or whips.

"This religious faith led to one of the most phenomenal events in religious history. When the fratricidal strife was on between the states, when brother sought the blood of brother and eleven states walked out of the Union, every man available went into the army. There was nobody left to run the plantations but the slaves and the mistress of the great house. She took these slaves and they ran the plantation . . . .

"For years the bloodletting went on. More than two million black men running the plantations under the direction of their mistress never for once took her life or molested her person. Such a story of loyalty's devotion was never before told nor since witnessed. They wouldn't molest that mistress. They knew in Hell they would wake up and they didn't want to go. A religious faith that carried with it a firm belief in the punishment for wrongdoing and a reward for righteous living bore fruit in this distressing hour.

"Quite different is the confused latterday delinquent who now has no dream of immortality or no faith of his own and who thinks supernatural and superstition are twin words and that the devil and Santa Claus are one person that's nobody but pa."

Then Judge Davidson addresses the nasty business of Emancipation, when Yankees who didn't know how to handle Africans came down and spoiled everything. "The Negro when treated kindly is one of the most loyal of all races. But there came an interruption. He was summoned up to the big house and told he was now free." Judge Davidson tells us that reaction of black people to their emancipation was to weep, "because they were parting from someone they loved."

"Pardon a personal reference here as it were, but such is the story that my grandmother has often told me. Just the other day we were talking to Honorable Neth Leachman, an outstanding member of the Dallas Bar. His grandparents were slaveholders in Harrison County near the City of Marshall and without knowing the story of my own grandmother he told me in identical language the story of his grandmother and how the slaves wept when freed."

Then came Reconstruction. "But the slave had a new leader; the carpetbagger came for entirely selfish reasons. He caused the Negro in so many ways to forget his God . . . ."

All so needless, if we just hadn't interrupted the smooth and morally superior workings of slavery, the judge broadly implies: "Referring again to the days of slavery, again I illustrate from my own family. My father and great-grandfather had many, many slaves. My great-grandfather built his slaves brick houses that they might be comfortable. He taught them to be good carpenters, to be good bricklayers as well as farmers. He used a Negro for foreman and never let a slave be whipped except upon his own orders."

123

There follows a long sort of rapture to Joe Louis, blacks on baseball diamonds, blacks in choirs singing "Swing Low Sweet Chariot" (". . . the very rafters would seem to rise and swell"), black people who are doing a lot better now than they were as slaves and all without benefit of "an act of Congress or a decree of a court."

Dipping back into yesterday again to find examples of racial systems that worked much better than what we have in the present, Judge Davidson tells us how very effective white Texans were during "the Tragic Era" (Reconstruction) at using terror to control the blacks. The directors of the Texas and Pacific Railroad became concerned when the predominantly black East Texas county of Harrison began electing black people to office when blacks were enfranchised briefly after the war. "Something must be done to save the county's credit. The county had voted a major bond issue as a promise to the T&P Railroad to locate its shops and general offices in Marshall. Those bonds of course would be worthless at maturity. Incidentally, I have one of those bonds which was subsequently paid and long after its liquidation came to me as a souvenir."

Judge Davidson, an operative of the Dallas Citizens Council, gives a peek into the historical genesis of these kinds of arrangements when he tells how the leaders of Marshall resolved their difficulties. "These men formed a group which afterwards was known as the Citizens Party. They made up a list of candidates for the county offices and drafted men to run.

". . . they persuaded some of the old-time darkies to stay away from the polls or go along with them and in some other cases they probably spread fear which would have involved them if we had had at that time a civil rights election law. The Citizens Party ticket won. The county taxes were properly allocated and apportioned.

". . . there has never been a bank failure in Harrison County."

This, in an opinion from the federal bench, is doubtless one of the most sweetly told tales of Ku Klux Klan violence anywhere in judicial literature. On the way from this story to his major point, Judge Davidson tosses in references to sex between black people and white people.

"When I was practicing law in Marshall a colored woman sought to employ me to sue her lodge. She stated that her lodge was designed to preserve the purity and integrity of the colored race . . . she had been unjustly expelled. . . . I didn't take the case, but I commended the purpose of the lodge.

"You walk along streets where the Negroes are more numerous than the whites, but you rarely see a mulatto child. An elderly darkie observing a mulatto child: 'He can't help it. I feel kindly toward him, but I don't think much of his mama and papa.' "

Davidson suggests that the wave of sex between black and white people brought on by desegregation will be so obnoxious to decent people that they will vacate a large portion of the nation, leaving behind a kind of mini-nation of miscegenists living in a band of "amalgamated spots stretching from the Potomac to the Brazos." But even this, a whole new country devoted to interracial sex, is not the ultimate horror keeping Judge Davidson awake at night. For that, we must move on to a section of his opinion called "Racial Integrity in History."

"In breeding a cow by linebreeding and care, you create a valuable animal, sometimes worth thousands of dollars. So linebreeding, if racial integrity is to be preserved, is something to be protected. In Southern Europe instead of linebreeding there has been cross-breeding. . . . Those who favor racial integrity do not look with favor upon the result. . . ."

From Southern Europe, we are swept into Biblical Egypt: "If the Ethiopians or even the Egyptians and the Hebrews had integrated and amalgamated during these 400 years there never would have been an exodus. There never would have been Ten Commandments handed down to their leader from Mt. Sinai."

So what would that have meant, we ask? Would we have had fourteen commandments? Nine? No, that's not the problem. The problem would be that, without an exodus, and without racially pure Jews, then Judas Maccabeus would never have established a colony on the shores of Lake Galilee, and "in this colony, Jesus Christ preached his sermon on the Mount."

Judge Davidson is explaining to us that Christianity itself is dependent on there being no sex between white people and black people. In fact, this "theory," purporting to give a theological basis for segregation and racial "purity," was being bandied about widely among white racists in Dallas at the time, making it no less remarkable to find it enshrined in Judge Davidson's opinion.

Given all this, it is an easily drawn conclusion for the judge to assert that, Brown v. Board of Education or no, real integration of the schools is an utter impossibility. "An old sage once remarked that your children will marry whomever they associate with and our army

125

life is proving that. .... Manifestly our Negro soldiers abroad have married white women."

School integration, Davidson says, "is in all probability the most direct and surest route to amalgamation which in the long run is the most objectionable of all features of integration. Integration rushes on to amalgamation."

In his conclusion, Judge Davidson broadly suggests that the Supreme Court probably doesn't really want real integration to occur, because it obviously wouldn't want to cause amalgamated spots to appear all over the country and thereby wipe out Christianity, so he recommends the old Morning News strategy of extreme tokenism accompanied by actual evasion. Judge Davidson suggests specific ways in which an order technically imposing desegregation on the schools could be evaded:

"Without purposely and intentionally discriminating between the races, you may for any good cause or reason assign pupils to schools other than that nearest them. Thus, to illustrate, if some pampered white boy, growing up without ever having been controlled or denied, enters an integrated school and by reason of his selfish propensities, pride or vanity or racial dislike creates a disturbance, he may be transferred to another school.

"Likewise, if an overgrown Negro boy in an integrated school should be by premature growth inclined to sex and should write verses on the blackboard of an obscene character designedly for the white girls to read or should make improper approaches to them so as to provoke trouble in the school, he should be assigned to a school where the situation is different."

The appeals court, which had been warning the Dallas bench that its opinions displayed "a total misconception of the constitutional rights asserted by the plaintiffs," finally came down hard on Davidson after this especially bizarre display and instructed him to order real desegregation of the schools for the following school year. In the order Davidson was finally forced to hand down, he began, "Never have we at any time entertained one unkind thought toward the colored race. My wet nurse as a child was a Negro woman." Then he warned black people against the sins of gloating.

"To the colored man, you are fully aware of having won in the courts of the land a history-making legal battle. If it calls for a triumph, remember the precept of General Grant at Appomattox: 'Never crow over the reverses of an honorable adversary'. .... It well behooves you to help avoid such untoward scenes and conditions as have prevailed in other cities."

He continued by denigrating the federal courts and his own order, which, he made clear, was not an expression of his own will, and by calling the principle of desegregation "un-American."

"Should a judge act when his conscience says no and where every sense of right and fair play says no, or should he under such conditions hold himself to be disqualified?

"To abolish a long-established social status or educational system by force is un-American. Such may be amicably done only by consent of the parties affected." He goes on to suggest that desegregation is being forced on Dallas by external and somehow foreign or alien forces: "The people of Dallas by 4 to 1 majority vote stand for segregation . . . . This unhappy controversy is not of our making. Our white people assuredly did not seek it. Our Negro friends and citizens did not start it. It is here, here by remote origin and control, one of many suits brought throughout the South. The man from afar understands not our problems as we do."

He finished by offering what was as close to an incitement of sedition as a federal judge could accomplish and stay on the bench: Judge Davidson urged that white people avoid violence but suggested strongly that his own order was not law.

"To the white man we would say that while every decision rendered by a Court does not become the law of the land yet, if the judgment so rendered puts in motion edicts of law and agencies of government, do not, though you disapprove, resort to violence in any form."

23

With this sort of help from the federal judge whose name was on the desegregation order, the task was that much more difficult for those leaders in Dallas who were sincerely committed to a peaceful transition. Some of the Citizens Council were smart enough to see that, even if the desegregation of businesses and public institutions could be ordered at fiscal gunpoint, the desegregating of the rank and file would take something more. Not that the typical job-holder in Dallas would be obstreperous. It was just that there were too many of them to call. Also, the solidity of leadership in Dallas had come apart a little in recent years. A lot of mixed signals had gone out, what with Criswell back in South Carolina calling for segregation of the religions, the Morning News predicting that the Supreme Court would forget about it after a while and Davidson's handing down opinions about how he had been nursed at the breast of a black woman. The leadership was supremely confident that Dallasites would do precisely what they were told to do. It was just a matter of finding an effective means of cutting through all the mixed signals and letting the troops know in dramatic and effective style what the marching orders were.

Since most of the people who were really interested in peace were merchants, they reached for a solution that came naturally to them — merchandising. "We engaged Sam Bloom — a public relations sage," Marcus said.

Desegregation would be marketed. Bloom, a former newspaper ad salesman who had founded his own advertising agency, was given the task of devising some sort of strategy. After some thought, Bloom came back to the council and proposed making a movie.

"He devised a concept," Marcus said, "which was that it wasn't fair to ask our children to take the brunt of the situation."

In the finished product delivered to C. A. Tatum of the Citizens Council, Bloom had achieved a masterpiece to stand the test of time. He had captured perfectly the voice of Dallas in 1961. The 20-minute movie, called *Dallas at the Crossroads,* was carried all over the city by Bloom and by members of the Citizens Council and was shown again and again, to neighborhood groups, discussion groups, schools, and, especially, it was shown to employees in firm after firm — people called into company auditoriums and lunchrooms and asked to sit while this important message was presented for their benefit and edification.

This passionate and political film tells the story of that moment. *Dallas at the Crossroads* is 20 minutes of image and sound that could only have come from Dallas, that could have swayed no other city as Dallas was swayed. We are not certain, when we take our chairs in the lunchroom, just what this "very important message" is all about, but we do as we are told, and wait quietly for it to begin. A rumor tells us it has to do with black people. The opening shot is of stained glass. We are swept to a hospital. A baby has been born and is being placed in its mother's arms. A deep brushy male voice tells us, "People are born in Dallas. The years that follow are filled with happiness ... (a long pause) ... and sadness."

All of a sudden, there is Big Tex, the giant statue of a cowboy that greets visitors to the State Fair. There is music, bouncy zingy string music of the sort we associate with newsreels about water skiing displays at Coral Gables.

A new voice, a brassy Walter Winchell voice, blares like a barker: "Dallas is a man-made town, and each man can find here an opportunity to make his life here whatever he wants." Now we're up over the Cotton Bowl and there's a big football game going on. "We call our town Big D, because it is big-hearted, open-handed, both friendly and progressive." Now we're at somebody's wedding. The music is pretty and soft. Now the couple is already out walking around a new subdivision, endless ranks of brick ranchettes.

"... for each man to learn, to play, to worship, for each man to own his own castle and achieve his own goals. Dallas is the finest home on earth to raise a family." (Here's a little white baby taking its first steps ... everybody's white so far, in fact ... no black people yet.)

"You work here. You have your home here. You raise your children here. Dallas lives and prospers through you, her people. The life of a city and its citizens are inseparable." The screen shows a bunch of Cub Scouts running around, people on patios, still all white, a baby crawling.

"With the passing of time, the faces of cities, like the faces of people, change." (Here's an old man in a rocking chair with another baby on his lap. The old man is turning toward us. He's going to talk now.)

"We want, we expect the face of Dallas to change," he tells us. "We just can't believe our city is as perfect as it is. I remember Dallas when. . . ."

... scenes of Armistice Day, the old Main-Street-when-it-was-a-sea-of-mud stuff.

"Change is not always easy," he says. (This must be the part about the black people.)

"As we change the face of Dallas, it is our responsibility to see that it is changed for the better, for what we have created ... we can also ... destroy." Accenting the verbal image, footage of a real tornado that had recently ripped through Oak Cliff fills the screen, gobbling up big buildings and spitting them out like garbage.

At this point, Walter Cronkite appears and is now in charge of the movie, dressed in black and back-lit against a black backdrop. With his young voice at its fullest and most orchestral, we begin a sort of travelogue, first visiting some places where there is no authority and everything is bad, and then moving to places where there is so much authority that we suspect, just sitting here on our metal chairs and looking at the screen, that we must be in some kind of very deep trouble ourselves.

In his very best newsy voice, Cronkite tells us: "On April 2, 1958, the face of Dallas was changed through natural disaster. A tornado appeared out of the blue, and for 40 minutes Dallasites watched it ravage through the city. But Dallas recovered."

Here are troops marching through a city. But it's not Dallas. It's Little Rock. In the next minute or so of film, Sam Bloom pulls out all the stops, and the merchants make their play.

"Other cities have faced, and faced recently, the same problems of change which Dallas now faces. They have met this problem with violence. The face of violence is the face of hate, unreason, cruelty, personal, and civic irresponsibility. Their actions and their results speak in these films for themselves."

Now we're in New Orleans, and what follows is several minutes of compelling, even riveting cinema. We could have sworn the tornado was going to be about black people, but instead they're showing us the twisted, bizarre, mouthing faces of white people, hating, hating intransitively, hating with their eyes and their breath and their bodies, white mobs screaming, a middle-aged woman's foot reaching up to kick a stranger, white men and women standing in mobs and shouting and gesturing angrily — a thoroughly terrifying vision of white America at its absolute worst.

Cronkite: "This is the face of man-made destruction. Its counterpart is the face of fear, bewilderment, suffering, physical and mental. This face can be a child's face. Your child's face." The frame is frozen. Inset behind a frozen Walter Cronkite is another frozen frame — a terrified white child in the arms of its screaming mother in the middle of a crazed mob.

So Sam Bloom and the merchants appealed to fundamental morality, to the desire of human beings not to become monstrous, and they did it by showing us our own monstrous potential.

The film then shows another view of the problem, and what follows is a succession of black-suited authority figures from the power structure explaining to people why they had better do what they are told to do, which is not have a riot. A law professor tells us about the law, ". . . a system where the unfortunate stand as peer and equal with the most privileged. . . . ," a judge (not Davidson) gives us some specifics on how the law will operate, should we make a big mistake and put ourselves before it, and then he makes sure, again, that we know what the deal is going to be in the specific matter of school desegregation:

"On April 6 of this year (1961), the federal court decision became final that some degree of desegregation must by law begin in Dallas this fall. In spite of arguments, in spite of criticism, in spite of personalities, the law is the law. Disagreement or dissatisfaction with any law should not and it must not be expressed by citizens in violence. In a democracy there are always legal channels open to persons who would prefer to change the law. These are the methods which a good citizen uses . . . (a long pause, a shake of the head, a stern glance) . . . not brickbats and stones."

Then Cronkite really gives it to us. The word, the bottom line: "On these principles Dallas stands. On these principles the leadership of

Dallas is firm. Through the Bar Association, the Medical Society, the Council of Churches, the Labor Council . . . from its elected officials, and its newspapers, Dallas has found many voices, but with a single message. . . ."

For the balance of the film, we travel from scene to scene, place to place, and everywhere we go there is a different man in a black suit telling us exactly and precisely what we will do. Mayor Earle Cabell tells us we will stand up and be counted for law and order. A minister, standing in front of that stained glass we saw at the opening, tells us: "You must be a good citizen." A labor leader, out in front of some big job site, reminds us that we "highly value active good citizenship and recognize fully the great influence that our city's good name has on job opportunities and a prosperous economy."

Standing in the middle of the city room at the Dallas Morning News, Ted Dealey tells us, "The editorial policy of the Dallas Morning News is to develop an atmosphere of nonviolence,"

Posed in front of a stream of newspapers racing on conveyors through the mailroom of the Dallas Times Herald, Managing Editor Felix McKnight makes the film's only direct reference to the morality of desegregation. "As a responsible newspaper, the Times Herald will not condone or tolerate impulsive actions of any individuals or group. We have only one basic elementary fact to face in preparation for the desegregation of our public schools. It is simple. It is just. It is realistic. It is mandatory."

Then, as we move up close to his face, McKnight tells us: "Our people must maintain unqualified respect for law and order."

It is for Cronkite, though, to hammer home the film's ultimate message and threat, here in the man-made city, here where fortunes bloom from a shoeshine and lives wither on a suspicious remark:

"There have always been a few individuals in every city . . . whose cure-all for any problem is to meet it with violence. In Dallas these few individuals . . . will . . . stand . . . alone."

And now we see a police car moving through the city. Police Chief Jesse Curry is telling us that he is going to get "those few who do not have the character and judgment to obey the law."

Then Curry tells us: "We know who these few are." The police are leading a white man into a cell. The door slams shut with a terrible heart-stopping clang. He is kneeling, bent and alone in the terrible shadows of his cell, broken with shame, his face fallen to the sink. He is ruined. He is finished. He is banished. In the distance, we hear the first notes of a choir. The ruined, banished man is fading from view.

Now the choir is singing the National Anthem, children are taking the pledge in a classroom, more white babies are being born, more white people are getting married to each other (never a black face in the whole movie), thousands of boy scouts, all white, are marching through downtown Dallas carrying hundreds of flags.

". . . and crown thy good, with brotherhood, from sea to shining sea."
Finis.

24

On September 6, 1961, the Dallas schools were desegregated with a calm and aplomb that was singled out for praise by everybody from President John F. Kennedy to The New York Times correspondent. The President called Dallas a "dramatic demonstration," with "law and order prevailing."

"In Dallas, Texas," he said in a statement at the end of the day, "the Citizens Council, working closely with Negro leaders, has shown how responsible, level-headed leadership can weld a whole community together to solve a difficult problem in race relations."

Gladwin Hill of the Times said, "You can usually sense tension in a community. Everything was so casual here. Dallas is that kind of town. The people here have a broader, more up-to-date attitude."

Of course, it was by then fully seven years after Brown v. the Board of Education; the Civil Rights Movement was hitting stride, exercising a good deal of pressure on the South to comply and making it plain to everyone what the consequences would be. Dallas was not alone that year in choosing discretion as the better part of valor. Another city singled out that fall for its exemplary compliance was Little Rock. There were others in Texas, Florida, Virginia, North Carolina and Tennessee that won the President's praise. The country generally was moving ahead. But, whatever went on elsewhere, nothing can detract from the sheer smoothness and efficiency of the day of reckoning in Dallas.

That morning, by the time the tune "School Days" began playing from the tower of Mr. Thornton's bank downtown, everyone was in his proper place, knew his cue and had memorized his lines. Wes Wise, who went on to buck the Citizens Council in the 1970s and get himself elected mayor, was a television reporter then. He says now that he and other reporters were chosen to cover the day's events because their superiors knew that they would do nothing to stir things up. Their instructions from their own editors were precise:

"We were to stand across the street from the main school where it was to take place, and we were told specifically, 'Don't cross that street. Don't cross that line.' At a particular time, we were free to take pictures, and the notebook and pencil guys could take notes.

"But it was all across the street. I don't know if you would have been able to pull that off or not now, but that was in a period when the old establishment was really in full power, and, as far as race relations and desegregating the public schools were concerned, it was really a blessing."

The police had posted signs all around City Park School, a white school in South Dallas, warning: "No Parking at Any Time," and "No Congregating or Loitering in this Area." But there was little need; the streets were strangely empty. The only onlookers when the first black children arrived were parents of other students, many of whom were Hispanic. In the tangled and ever-changing web of racial-tribal definition and identity, Hispanics at that time were considered white, and the Anglo community was already beginning a tradition of trying to use the mixing of black and Hispanic students to satisfy the courts.

But, if the Anglo majority still had tricks up its sleeve, the evolving consciousness of the minorities was not far behind. Watching the black kids arrive with their parents, Mrs. Rita Cruz, a Mexican national who only had been in town a few months, said, "In Mexico there is no distinction between race. We need this in this country. I was refused service in a bus station on my way to Dallas, because they said I was 'colored.' I know how they feel, and besides, my husband says this is nothing to get alarmed about."

Raymundo Roman, a tailor in a downtown men's store, said, "Remember, they are humans, and if the law is to come, it must come. I have only boys. Someone with girls might object, though."

Thus, little Flora Nell Pitts, a first-grader whose ancestors had come to North America from Africa, was allowed to enter City Park School wearing a starched tan and yellow checked dress and yellow socks. Around the city, other black children slipped into schools through side doors or marched up the front walk gripping the hands of their parents, and a small portion of the spell was broken.

That same day, the black men who had sat on the biracial committee and helped construct this pageant received a political slap and suffered still more erosion of credibility in their own community. Superintendent W. T. White withdrew a promise that more black students would be allowed to transfer to white schools later in the term, making it plain on the very first day that what had been accomplished was tokenism and that the school district would countenance nothing more, no matter what promises had been made to avoid a riot. Two days later, a five-foot-high wooden cross, wrapped in quilts and soaked in gasoline, was ignited on the lawn of Lisbon Elementary School. But these things were deemed small at the time by the larger white community. That the capacity for Klan-style violence was still out there somewhere and that the great racial progress the city had achieved was to be ceremonial, not real, were surprises to no one. It was a whole lot better than anyone had expected.

Certainly, the ritual desegregating of the schools did not entail changing the important and time-honored practices in Dallas by which land and money were stolen from black people under color of law. The post-war morality of "urban renewal," tempered by time in most other cities by then, had not softened at all in Dallas in the 1960s. A black neighborhood that had become surrounded by white neighborhoods was still treated by whites as an obvious physical blight, like a swamp or a dirty creek that needed to be "corrected" in the interest of the larger public good.

A black neighborhood north of Northwest Highway near White Rock Lake had become surrounded by expensive new white-owned homes. The neighborhood, on land deeded in 1865 to former slaves, Jeff and Hanna Hill, was called "Little Egypt" by the residents, who had named their church the "Little Egypt Baptist Church," because the neighborhood and the church were associated with deliverance from bondage.

In 1962, Dallas Morning News readers snickered over a tongue-in-cheek headline, "200 Little Egypt Residents to Leave 'Bondage.'" The story, by Larry Grove, explained how the entire neighborhood had been "discovered" when realtor Adrene Bailey of McFarland & Cash Real Estate "first noticed" it across the road from Northlake Shopping Center. She became the intermediary for a syndicate of white investors. On the day when trucks showed up to haul the black families out, Ms. Bailey told Grove she was pleased that "everything went so well."

Sarah Robinson, one of the trustees of the Little Egypt Baptist Church, said she had decided it was time to give up the land before "condemnation proceedings that residents could ill afford."

Grove's story said that a "fashionable shopping center" was to be built on the land. The families who had lived there since Emancipation were to take their money, "a minimum of $6,500 per family," and scatter themselves to the winds. School desegregation had done nothing to slacken the avarice of white people gazing on black-owned land.

For all the pride the white establishment continues to take today in the peaceful 1961 "desegregation" of the schools, few black people in Dallas remember it as a major milestone or harbinger of real change in their lives. Most blacks who were around at the time say the real changes didn't start until after the assassination. If anything, the right-wing extremist fever that had begun brewing in the white community in the mid-fifties seemed to whirl and burn even brighter after 1961, as if the ceremonial depurifying of the white schools had unleashed a seething wrath, and it was not until John Kennedy had been murdered in Dealey Plaza and the world's wrath turned on Dallas, that the inner furies in the white community were defeated, or at least subdued once more.

Immediately after the token desegregation of the schools, some black people in Dallas — by no means all — began finally to push for real desegregation. The encouragement that the Kennedy brothers had given black people and white liberals, their defense of the freedom riders, and their respect for Martin Luther King had boosted the morale of the Civil Rights Movement.

The anger that this new aggressiveness by blacks aroused in the white establishment in Dallas was immediately snarled together with a bitter hatred of the Kennedys. In denouncing them, The Dallas Morning News, chief organ of the anti-Kennedy, antiblack claque in Dallas, dragged out some of the old conservative antispending lore that had been in mothballs since the rule of FDR. But spending and economic policy were not what was making the far right wing in Dallas hate the Kennedys. Those were not principal causes. The principal cause was race.

Dallas had believed it would be done with the race question when it had, as the Morning News had urged in the beginning, achieved a technical compliance with the orders of the courts. It was when the black struggle moved beyond tokenism that the real white resistance began, and it began with the realization that what was afoot was fundamental social and political change, not mere ceremony. Even before President Kennedy had won the election, the white establishment in Dallas, whose practice had been to allow people to vote yes or no for the Citizens Council slate in city elections, developed a sudden concern about what was called "bloc" voting, which really meant black voting.

Dr. L. G. Pinkston, one of the oldest and most trusted of the white leadership's liaisons in black Dallas and a member of the various biracial committees since 1941, assured his white Republican friends before the election in 1960 that the apparent affection of black people for the Kennedys had only shallow roots, that there wouldn't be much real voting and that the only thing black people hoped for from them anyway was patronage: "Now, if the Democrats should win, they can go to them and say, 'Look what we did for you. How about a government job?' "

C. B. Bunkley, Jr. was less accommodating of white fears. He predicted black people in Dallas would vote for Kennedy and against Nixon by about three-to-one. He was right. After the election, a single headline in the Morning News told readers all they needed to know: "Negro Votes Credited for JFK Win."

In the months and years ahead, as conscience and the tidal pull of history drew the Kennedy administration closer and closer to the black struggle, the Kennedys excited an ever more intense and thickly woven welter of race hatred and xenophobia in Dallas, and in all of Texas. The tension over civil rights was splitting the liberal and conservative wings of the Democratic Party in Texas — a state Kennedy had barely won in 1960 and probably could not be reelected without in 1964. It was this rift that brought him to Dallas, and to his death, in 1963. By that time, the welcome waiting for him in Dallas was so vile that several advisers and friends had begged him not to come.

The Dallas Morning News, under a different generation of leadership today and a vastly changed and improved journal for it, was then a primary agent of the special fury that had enveloped Dallas. The city seemed to have attracted every loosely wound right-wing nut case in eighteen states. In addition to the Minutemen, Minutewomen and John Birchers already thronging the cocktail party circuit, more sinister free-lance troublemakers like General Edwin Walker of Ole

Miss fame were coming to town, zanies and gun collectors of the right and the left, and some who seemed to flip both ways, like Lee Harvey Oswald. But the poison was also general and socially acceptable, as Klan loyalty had been in Dallas 40 years earlier.

"I found it very difficult to go to a dinner party," Stanley Marcus remembered, "without getting into violent discussions. If you disagreed, you were automatically labeled a communist.

"It was a hostile, know-nothing atmosphere — the atmosphere that resulted in the election of Bruce Alger as a congressman.

Marcus lays much of the blame for that atmosphere — and for national tragedy it produced — at the lintel of The Dallas Morning News. "The News, of course, has changed 180 degrees since then, and I think it's a fine newspaper now, but I have always charged that The Dallas Morning News then was as responsible and as answerable as any single institution, because they never repudiated it."

25

Far from repudiating the violent extremism of the period, the editorial page of The Dallas Morning News wove an idiosyncratic texture of race-baiting and phobic anti-Kennedy feeling that set the tone for much of what happened in Dallas during that period. It was the voice of great new wealth that has not yet learned responsibility, of raw power, new and mean, untempered by civilization, red in tooth and claw. Many Morning News editorials of the period read like the voice of someone who wasn't sober when he wrote them, using a lot of the very same obfuscation and clumsy euphemism that Judge Davidson was handing out over at the federal building.

The Morning News editorials presented a consistent theme: that communism, far from having anything to do with arrangements of property or means of production, was a matter of encouraging insolence among black people. The Morning News presented its readers with a clear exposition in mid-July 1963.

The top of the editorial page is dominated by a cartoon in which a shifty-looking Robert Kennedy holds a mirror and wonders, "Mirror, mirror, what's my fate? Will I be it in '68." The lead editorial complains, "The President continues to insist that, in the nation's racial crises, 'We are confronted primarily with a moral issue.' He has not elaborated, as the plaintiff in a legal case should, so he leaves himself open to questions."

The editorial warns that mixing moral issues with politics is pretty risky business, but, as long as the Kennedys started it, how about these issues:

"Is it moral to follow the communist line, which is an atheistic, Godless line? (The American Communisty Party long has advocated what Mr. Kennedy now asks the Congress to approve as civil rights bills.)

"Is it moral to lend indirect support to the forces of disorder and violence — many of which forces have communist front affiliations?

"Is it moral to take a man's income tax and, without his permission, spend it abroad as 'foreign aid' in countries which deny the existence of a Supreme Creator and imprison those who want to worship as they please?

"Is it moral to 'manage' news, when the American people have a right to truth?

"Is it moral to foster inflationary policies which reduce the value of insurance and annuities that people invested in for their security? Is this any different from stealing out of their pockets?

"Is it moral to protect statutes that encourage women to bear children out of wedlock?

"Is it moral to permit laggards and the indolent to loaf half the year on unemployment compensation while the conscientious continue to work for a living?

"Trust us, nearly every problem in this country can be interpreted as a 'moral issue.' The racial struggle is no more entitled to this exclusive designation than aid to communist Tito or compulsory unionism."

Even with the deepest reverence we can summon today for the first amendment and for a free exchange of ideas, it is nevertheless still breathtaking to read these diatribes, in which a major metropolitan daily newspaper accuses the President of the United States and his family of treason and subversion, and it is more breathtaking to realize that the community to which these words were addressed, for the most part, read them and nodded its serene assent.

As much as the Morning News reviled the Kennedys, they still were not the heart of its message. The heart of the message was that black people who gazed straight into white eyes and spoke their minds without deference, who made demands and behaved as if they were the equals of whites, were communists. When the Morning News wasn't saying it directly, it put its message across by bending the news columns mercilessly to reflect its racist editorial policy or by playing games with juxtaposition of copy.

In June 1963, The Dallas Morning News presented Martin Luther King's moving "letter from Birmingham jail" by sandwiching it on the editorial page between two other items. Above King's letter was a long paean to the Confederacy and segregation by the chancellor of the University of Mississippi. King's letter followed, ending on a resounding and uplifting chord:

"One day the South will know that when these disinherited children of God sat down at lunch counters they were in reality standing up for the best in the American dream and the most sacred values in our Judeo-Christian heritage, and thusly carrying our whole nation back to those great wells of democracy which were dug deep by the founding fathers in the formulation of the Constitution and the Declaration of Independence."

Then, directly beneath King's closing phrase, a bold headline: COMMIES AND NEGROES, an editorial reprinted from the Albany Times-Union about how black people are mistreated in communist countries: "So, Radio Moscow, how about beaming this news back to Africa?"

The atmosphere in Dallas was not merely fractious. It was physically terrifying, so much so that, after the Morning News worked over Arkansas Senator J. William Fulbright, he declined invitations of friends in Dallas and told them he was physically afraid to come. Lyndon Johnson and his wife were attacked physically and spat upon by a group of Republican women in Dallas and, for years afterward when she thought about returning to Dallas, Mrs. Johnson's hands made nervous fists; Adlai Stevenson, the nation's ambassador to the United Nations, was attacked in Dallas in an atmosphere reminiscent of Nixon in Caracas.

Stanley Marcus was with Stevenson on October 24, 1963, when the mob surrounded him. To this day, his eyes widen when he calls the scene to mind. "I pushed him into the car, and they surrounded us. They were rocking the car."

That kind of hate-fever in Dallas during the years just before the assassination was repaid in kind in the years after it. To this day, Dallasites still have to get to know a newcomer fairly well before they'll really talk about what it was like to be from Dallas afterward. Every white native Dallasite of the period has some emblematic memory — toll money hurled back from a booth on a New Jersey turnpike, room service that didn't include guests from Dallas and much worse. The sentiment has not faded entirely to this day.

The city spent a fortune to host the 1984 Republican Convention because, 21 years later, it was still trying hard to do something that would erase the memory, lock the file, change the verdict. Ironically, by 1984 the memory Dallas had tried so hard to outlive had lived on in Dallas while it had faded elsewhere. To its surprise, Dallas found that, while no one had forgotten and some still had misgivings about the city, the rest of the country associated it more with a television soap opera and a professional football team than with the death of a president.

The men of the Citizens Council suffered an enormous shock when Kennedy was assassinated. Yet it wasn't simply that a president had been killed in their midst. They began immediately saying that it could have happened anywhere. They weren't shocked that the killing had wrought anger and pain. From the day of the frontier, it had always been a tenet of western faith that life, all life, even good life is built upon a foundation of anger and pain. No, that was the predictable aftermath of a terrible crime and a stroke of real bad luck, like a tornado crashing through Oak Cliff. These things weren't what shocked the men who believed they had built up Dallas with their own hands, that they had created something from nothing, a city of enormous and powerful concrete things from a mortar of sheer willpower.

The shock was that ideas were on the verge of pulling down everything they had built. The levees, the dams, the industrial districts and office towers; all of it could stop cold and die, all because of ideas, bad ideas, mere ideas. For all the effort the business community had invested in control, the crazies had grown worse and worse. In response, the oligarchy would attempt to exert even more control, never glimpsing the circularity of the problem. No one had less experience of or trust in democracy, after all, than the oligarchs, and that had been the beginning of the fall.

Not long before the assassination, Congressman Henry B. Gonzalez of San Antonio had come to Dallas to receive an award from the local chapter of the NAACP. The presentation was made in a small Baptist church. Gonzalez, whose district was famous for wide-open rough-and-tumble American-style politicking, was baffled by the mood of the ceremony. His hosts were noticeably nervous, almost physically afraid; they shoved a plaque into his hands and departed quickly into the night. When he got back to Washington, Gonzalez made a joke of it to the President.

"Dallas is like the Congo," he said. "It isn't ready for self-government."

How could it be? There hadn't been any real self-government in Dallas in 30 years. The ideas that were putting the entire enterprise at risk weren't the paranoid fantasies of the Minutewomen, at least not at bottom. Those ideas were only symptomatic of the more fundamental failing, the failure to allow people to engage the machinery of government themselves, freely, individually, any way they felt like engaging it, to take over City Hall, or get a neighbor fined for letting his weed crop grow too tall. All of the people needed to be able to put their hands on the machine and feel how it moved when the urge was upon them.

Only now has Dallas even started to be able to admit to itself what it worked so hard to deny and repress all those years: that Dallas did kill Kennedy. Not deliberately, not conspiratorially. For years, the Dallas Morning News was so eager to prove that nobody in Dallas had been in on it that the paper became the main engine driving the cult of conspiracy theory surrounding the assassination, passing on any and every conspiracy theory it could lay its hands on, as long as the conspirators in the theory hadn't been members of the Citizens Council. Only now has the city cooled enough to see that conspiracy never was the issue. The issue was the one Dallas had started with, the one Dallas had thought was its private domain and specialty — civic responsibility.

Marcus says now, "I remember also that, following the assassination, there was a great desire on the part of the leadership to cope with the situation. The word cope was the way to describe it. And everyone was saying, 'Well, it could have happened anywhere.'

"Of course that was true. But it did happen here, and it happened partially because of the atmosphere that attracted that kind of fanatic nut. And when a community doesn't do anything to express disapprobation, it is logical that it will attract more and more of them."

26

Black people in Dallas took the murder of John Kennedy as a direct, personal, and racial assault, a heartbreaking blow, like a death in the family or a divorce, part of the unbroken fabric, the unwavering line that reached up out of the traditions of the 19th century and still flared on crosses on the lawn, bombs thrown from cars, and beatings. Eddie Bernice Johnson said, "Just before the assassination, it seemed to me no matter how hard we tried, there was such a prevailing hatred of black people in Dallas. It was depressing. When the assassination came, I took it personally. To me, I thought he was being killed because he was one of the first national leaders who stood up for equality.

"I did not sleep for days. A president was killed because he was trying to make us equal. That feeling made me so miserable. If there was any opportunity to join any group, I took it.

"What I saw after, I saw in my judgment that it was clear that blacks were not going to take this any more peacefully. But it was clear that the Dallas leaders were not going to have overt rioting. After that, it was like putting out fires."

Putting out fires. The phrase comes up again and again when black Dallasites who lived through the period talk about the oligarchy in the years after Kennedy was killed. Dr. Charles Hunter, a sociologist at Bishop College in Dallas, says, "I would describe the Citizens Council during that period as a very efficient fire department."

Race relations in other cities of the nation may have been adrift at that time, in Detroit, in Los Angeles and Newark. White leaders in other American cities may have been asleep at the wheel. But not in Dallas. Lee Harvey Oswald had seen to that. The oligarchy was all too painfully aware that things were bad in Dallas, potentially very bad, and it was galling that there should be such disarray after all the effort the leadership had invested in order. The white leadership was very alert and ready to act, ready to do whatever was necessary to quell trouble before it could flare out of control. If it meant negotiation, there would be negotiation. If it meant head busting, there would be head busting.

The oligarchy knew exactly where to watch for the trouble to start. Black demands, civil rights, the Kennedys: It had all been of one string. Perhaps nowhere in America was the attention of white leaders focused so intently on the black community as in Dallas following the assassination. Born of arrogance, guilt, and genuine concern for the city, this sense of urgency worked on the black community in a number of ways. Where the relationship had been authoritarian, as in the linkage of the black ministerial alliance and the Citizens Council, it became more so. In the years after the assassination, traditional black leaders were called upon to run errands that were more and more transparently the will of the white power structure. But at the same time, important changes were taking place in the white community. The real fear of uprising that even the oligarchy felt at that time tended to make white power-wielders more flexible, if and where they thought flexibility was what would work.

A whole new white population, meanwhile, was arriving on the scene and beginning to make waves, an unforeseen political wage the oligarchy had to pay for all its brilliant success in booming the city. Many of the new white people were relatively liberal — that is, they were certain that slavery had been morally wrong, they were not certain that Reconstruction had been the worst atrocity in the history of the planet, and they believed the rule of law and the rights of property should extend uniformly to all Americans no matter what their physical appearance — all of which markedly distinguished the newcomers from the entrenched white power structure in Dallas. All of these white people had been absolutely galvanized by the horror of the assassination.

While race relations in other American cities were in a kind of deaf and dumb historical float, drifting relentlessly to the brink, race relations in Dallas were the object of intense and thoughtful management, of white domineering on the one hand and white liberal compassion on the other, but all of it much more aggressively and pointedly addressed than white sentiment elsewhere. The ability of black people to search for and find moderates in the white community obligated the old immoderates on the Citizens Council to soften their act. The end product was that, once again, Dallas pitched itself away from its predilection for extremism and leaned heavily instead into its talent for accommodation.

The year after the assassination, Reverend Zan Wesley Holmes, Jr., 29-year-old black pastor of the 650-member Hamilton Park Methodist Church and a graduate of the Perkins School of Theology at Southern Methodist University in Dallas, was elected president of the Dallas Pastors Association, the white counterpart of the black community's ministerial alliance. At the same time, the pastors association elected a Roman Catholic to its board for the first time.

Holmes, young and bright, a scholar, smooth, morally sure of himself, intellectually spirited but eminently reasonable in debate, was a typical product of Hamilton Park and was typical of the new leadership emerging in the black community. Within a month of his installation as head of the previously all-white Pastors Association, Holmes was out on the speakers' trail, explaining black folks to white folks and getting right down to the basics in ways that a less polished emissary could not have accomplished. He told a racially mixed audience in suburban Richardson, just across the line from Hamilton Park, that black Americans wanted justice, not sex with white people. "We want to be your brothers, not your brothers-in-law," he said.

"We don't consider intermarriage with whites a badge of honor or distinction. We don't want to get a stranglehold on society to repay it for past prejudices. We don't expect special privileges which would be denied to others. We want the common courtesy accorded any human being. We don't want to be called 'Boy.' We want to be judged by character, not by color. We expect to be given and to assume that share of responsibility which is ours to improve ourselves."

Looking back on those years now, Holmes sees his election to the presidency of the pastors association and his larger role in the community as directly connected with the assassination. "I became president in the year immediately following the assassination of President Kennedy, and there was a strong relationship there. Dallas had this sensitivity, the guilt, wanting to demonstrate that it was indeed the All-American City."

147

"But one of the most significant things that happened after the Kennedy assassination was that new white groups that challenged the conservative leadership began to emerge. People seemed to have a serious mission to turn Dallas around. Those were exciting days."

The hovering attentions of the white community did not produce equally exciting results in all quarters of the black community. While the era just after the Kennedy assassination may have been a boom time for those black leaders who naturally found alliance and sympathy among white liberals, the period of the middle and late 1960s was a tragic one for the traditional leadership of the black community, many of whom had fought the good fight in earlier decades. For all of the bending going on in some quarters, the boot was coming down in others; chits were called due, and the black accommodationists who had always led their community in the past simply were not equipped personally, philosophically or morally to deal with the pressure.

The year 1964 was the fulcrum on which the decade was forged. The Reverend Ira B. Loud, pastor of St. Paul Methodist Church and a totemic figure in the Interdenominational Ministerial Alliance, sounded the black establishment's theme for the year in April, when he angrily denounced student demonstrations at all-black Huston-Tillotson College in Austin:

"It was a sad day when the students of Huston-Tillotson College chose to demonstrate," Loud told his flock. "Even though they were misguided by a white faculty member, the local NAACP and a few transient freedom riders, the administration and their parents have a right to expect them to think.

"I do not actually know what the segregation-integration climate in Austin is. I do know they were not sent to college to change the current situation in Austin. I also know that the cities in Texas have been working overtime to establish a policy of fairness in employment, accommodations, etc. to people of all races.

"The rapid progress which is being made in the cities in Texas in race relations can be seen by all, except those whose ingratitude has blinded them. It is the depth of ingratitude for any students who are recipients of scholarships and other financial aid to demonstrate against their school when they know they are biting the very hand which is feeding them."

It can be argued that there were tragic figures like Loud in every city in the nation but that they were exceptions to the rule, men and women who had served their people well and courageously in earlier times and other contexts but who had made the mistake of living too long. Unfortunately, in Dallas, Ira B. Loud was no exception.

Dr. Ernest C. Estell, the black pastor who had called the white man's bluff on the bombings of the early 1950s and who had been an important and effective battler for the end of ritual segregation, was in 1964 an unhappy example of what happened to many black leaders in Dallas in the sixties. In the rest of the nation in 1964, an important divergence was taking place in the black struggle. The older tradition of the freedom rides and the voter registration drives in the South was giving way to a much more violent, wrathful, and revolutionary energy in the Northern cities. The efforts of the organized Civil Rights Movement in the South were concentrated as never before in the "Freedom Summer" mobilization in Mississippi, sponsored mainly by CORE and SNNC. In the North, where gangs of black kids were jeering Martin Luther King and calling him an Uncle Tom, the first of the urban uprisings were beginning to occur. Malcolm X. had just formed the black Nationalist Party and white liberals often were not welcome at the black table.

Much of the white South was seething that year over the passage of civil rights legislation, proposed by the murdered President and achieved by his successor, the president from Texas. In the course of the Freedom Summer drive in Mississippi, 85 civil rights workers were beaten, more than 1,000 were arrested, 37 black churches and 31 black-owned homes were burned and blown to bits, some of them bombed from overhead by bag-dropping rednecks in the "Klan Air Force." Three of the volunteer voter registration workers were martyred: Michael H. Schwerner, 24, of Brooklyn, Andrew Goodman, 20, of New York, and James E. Chaney, 21, of Meridian, Mississippi.

The Congress of Racial Equality in Dallas had staged a number of sit-ins and peaceful actions to protest the ongoing and illegal formal segregation of many of the city's restaurants and the almost total actual segregation of the schools that followed ritual desegregation. Concentrating their efforts on the Piccadilly Cafeteria at 1503 Commerce, CORE officials made it plain that, as much as their efforts were a response to white racism in Dallas, they were also a response to what they considered to be the failure of traditional black leadership.

One of the leaders of the Piccadilly protests, Rev. Earl E. Allen, called the Piccadilly protests "an outgrowth of our failure to reach some type of agreement with the Dallas School Board, plus the fact we have not been able to get some type of understanding with the power structure of the city. We used this method of dramatizing the fact that Dallas is not the harmonious city that the leaders say it is. There is a great deal of racial discrimination in the city of Dallas."

White people in Dallas at that time, even some liberals, didn't believe it. There was an enormously smug assumption that the end of formal segregation of the schools had been miracle enough for one century and that racism was, for the most part, a creature of the past. Dallas was beginning to feel sophisticated. Now the city even had some modern art in the museum. At the annual Gridiron Show of the Dallas Press Club — to this day a telling and not very encouraging barometer of racism in the city — the local press got together over drinks and behind closed doors with the white leadership, and everyone hooted and howled when the people in the stage skits sang, to the tune of "Nothing like a Dame":

"We've got 8-foot Abyssinians who can open up the door; we've got portraits of Dmitri 'til they're hanging on the floor. . . .," and, to the tune of "Love in Bloom," "When e'er we learn that questions burn, and problems overhead loom, oh no, we don't get concerned; we call Sam Bloom."

This is not to say no effort was made to understand what black people were saying in the streets. In the second week of August, The Dallas Morning News introduced a series that attempted to discover what was on the minds of black people. An introduction tells us that "The News obtained the services of a Negro to help with the interviews."

The first person quoted is an unnamed black. The name is not important, we are told, because "Across the board, rich and poor . . . their answers were nearly unanimous."

The subject of the interview, an unnamed but presumably unanimous black person, tells us, "The Negro is a hard animal to understand. He has been down so long he does not know how to act in association with whites. He is profane, a sure sign of weakness of character. He talks too loud. These are some of the reasons he has not been accepted. Often he seeks his rights but forgets his responsibilities of full citizenship."

The oligarchy may have chuckled at the typically fawning humor tossed its way by the Dallas press corps at the Gridiron dinner, but, back in the office, the men who really ran things had their eyes wide open. There were stirrings of violence already. Thirteen white people surrounded six blacks at White Rock Lake one night, and the black people shot their way out of it, killing a white man. In other incidents, a black motorist shot and wounded a white man but escaped before anyone could get his side of the story. A melee broke out between blacks and whites outside Memorial Auditorium following a black pop concert. The protests continued downtown. Did any of it mean anything? Was some large threat moving again out there on the border, trying to get in?

27

In early August, John McKee, president of the Dallas Crime Commission, announced the official policy of the city's unelected leaders, that "protestors" would be treated as "common criminals." The terms were important usages of the period. The term "protestor" meant not all people who protest but certain people, a certain type associated with the Civil Rights Movement then, people who would become involved in the antiwar movement within a few years, black people and young white people, not yet called hippies, who protested things the crime commission did not want to have protested. If you were a "common criminal," as opposed to being a criminal, that meant you were really going to get your head kicked in.

On the night of August 22, 1964 — what had been an ordinary night until that moment, another in the endless string of nights that make the life of a city — the driveway doors cranked open at police garages in substations all over Dallas, and 200 officers organized in special "strike forces" came roaring out to inflict "Operation Crime Slow-Down" on certain hot spots.

The special strike forces linked up with the normal night patrols already on duty and began a campaign of stop-and-frisk shakedowns, a clear violation of constitutional rights.

Dallas Police Chief Jesse Curry urged decent citizens who found themselves accidentally caught in the net to be understanding of the larger need being served: "We realize that respectable citizens will be stopped. But it's not always possible for our officers to recognize a good citizen from a police character by their dress. These citizens have no need to worry if they are on legitimate business."

In this effort to awe the black community with the brute force of the police department, Dr. Ernest C. Estell was a vital and very visible element. Speaking for the Interdenominational Ministerial Alliance, Estell announced that an end was being called to all tactics of political confrontation.

"Picketings, sit-ins, wade-ins, lie-ins and similar methods of direct action have reached and passed their peaks of effectiveness as instruments for the promotion of civil rights," Estell said. Estell made it especially clear that the racial committee, now called the Dallas Community Committee, had nothing to do with CORE or with any of the summer's activities.

"We wish to dissociate ourselves as a Negro community with anything that borders on impropriety. The impression has been given that the DCC and similar organizations were working (with CORE), and they were not."

The Morning News devoted an editorial to Dr. Estell's good sense, invoking the paper's favorite theory of foolish self-seeking politicians, black and Irish, who provoked the beast and then could not control it: ". . . the leaders who started it all by trying to outdo each other in militancy now have lost control in many cases to the most dangerous extremists, the black racists and communists."

But The Dallas Morning News wasn't Estell's only admirer. Nor were all of his believers white. There were historically important cadres in the black community who ignored the accommodationists of this period and called them Uncle Toms, but the black community at large listened to men like Loud and Estell. The demonstrations didn't come to a halt, but the level of confrontation definitely slacked. The wind went out of the movement. In Dallas, peace was still more valuable than progress.

One year later, on August 11, 1965, a California highway patrolman attempted to arrest a young black motorist at the intersection of Avalon Boulevard and Imperial Highway in Los Angeles; a crowd gathered; tempers flared, and Watts went up in raging flames. A Los Angeles Times reporter wrote: "The rioters were burning their city now, as the insane sometimes mutilate themselves."

An essential point the Los Angeles Times writer failed to see or to weigh sufficiently, however, was that some of the black people taking part in or even merely witnessing the riot did not view it as madness, but as the ultimate and long overdue return of sanity. By this view of things, the shredding, looting, and burning of the city was the ultimate sanction against an ultimately unjust society. The Watts riot was a horrible, ruthless statement. It said: if there is not going to be justice in this society, there is not going to be a society.

Writing after the Watts riot, Dr. Frederick J. Hacker, a black physician and an advisor to the Westminster Neighborhood Association, the largest black social welfare agency in Watts, said: "For the Negroes, what happened in southeastern Los Angeles in August was justified legally and morally. Where the police saw black criminals tearing apart law and order with a cascade of Molotov cocktails, the Negroes of Watts watched freedom fighters liberating themselves with blood and fire. The McCone Report says that only two percent of the Negroes participated in the rioting. It implies that the rest of the Negro community was cowering in darkened houses waiting for the forces of law and order to rescue them. Actually, the majority of the 400,000 Negroes in the area supported the riots. As one high-school girl said afterwards, 'Every time I looked out my window and saw another fire, I felt new joy.'

"For the Negroes, there was no reason to feel guilt, shame or regret . . . they felt the looting and burning were merely excesses of a just cause and thus justified. In that respect, the Watts riots were psychologically analogous to the Hungarian Revolution and the Boston Tea Party. . . . As in the mythology of bullfighting, violence — the ultimate violence that could or does lead to death — is the great unifier, the strange symbol of reality confronted with an ultimate truth. When one is nakedly facing one's destiny, presumably all falsehood and pretense falls away and one is — as described by rioters — 'close to God.' "

This is the cleansing, invigorating, heady sense of which Frantz Fanon had written in Algeria in the 1950s and 1960s, the lightning that occurs when dark-skinned people throw off the cloak of make-believe, the shuffling, dissembling disguise they have worn to ward off beatings and bombs, the smiles that had to be smiled to hold on to whatever crust had been granted, to survive. The rioter, by this school of thought, is not a rioter but a human being recapturing his full humanity, demanding that the city see him and know that he can be death and destruction, that he is a necessary ingredient, a human being who can pull the plug on the whole operation and will, if pressed.

Dr. Hacker concluded: "There was an extraordinary religious —

almost mystical — fervor. Economic and social injustices took on religious meaning. . . . The injustices had betrayed the promises of the Bible that all people should be equal and that the lowest is as good as the highest. Watts stood for every deprived Negro community. Frequently there was overt identification with Christ as a sacrificial being who by his suffering takes upon himself and atones for the sins of everybody."

Fanon had preached violence as a sort of self-help program for the oppressed. "At the level of individuals, violence is a cleansing force," Fanon said in his *Wretched of the Earth,* a sixties manual. "It frees the native from his inferiority complex and from his despair and inaction; it makes him fearless and restores his self-respect."

There was a literary and political aesthetic of rioting in the 1960s, celebrated by writers such as Aime Cesaire: "We had attacked, we the slaves; we, the dung underfoot, we the animals with patient hooves.

"We were running like madmen; shots rang out . . . . We were striking. Blood and sweat cooled and refreshed us. We were striking where the shouts came from, and the shouts became more strident and a great clamor rose from the east: It was the outhouses burning and the flames flickered sweetly on our cheeks."

Many people, black and white, would reject out of hand the assertion that there is anything dignified or even political in rioting and looting. Alex Bickley, the recently retired director of the Citizens Council, looked back through time and explained his theory of the riot in Detroit in 1967, a city he visited in search of just such answers:

"I went to Detroit right after the riot. I walked and talked about it. I was lucky, I picked up an individual who owned a lot of property in there where it happened. He pointed it all out to me. He'd say, 'There's a business that served these folks well, but everybody had a charge account there. These were the businesses that were burned down.' "

In this view, then, the riots had no moral or social or psychological roots or role: They were simple larceny. A terrible, enormous larceny, but only larceny — the thieving of the fruits of civilization and labor. Blacks rioted to get out of paying on their charge accounts.

The point here isn't even which version of the riots is the correct one. The point is that many of the black people in cities where there were riots believed they were experiencing something momentous and important. If nothing else, they looked in white eyes and saw fear, and they knew that they had put it there.

28

hite people in Dallas have never feared black people, because white people have never lost control. That is not to say that white people in Dallas never have had compassion for black people. That's a different matter.

In fact, by the 1960s, the growth of the Dallas economy, envisioned and nurtured by the levee gang, had produced a new kind of money crop in electronics, and with the new technology had come an entire new element in the white community.

Especially centered around the vastly successful Texas Instruments company, there were large numbers of white people coming to Dallas who often had not lived with formal segregation and who placed great value on education and intellectual attainment. Erik Jonsson, the mayor whose tenure saw the early transition from dependent to independent power in the black community, came to city hall in the sixties from T.I., where he had been an early captain and tycoon. The T.I. presence in Dallas politics came along almost immediately as the only real moment for rioting passed, sweeping the black commuity into an engulfing, if temporary, relationship with white liberals before there was time for mischief.

Jonsson was more willing than the oligarchy of the early fifties had been to speak to and even deal with black Dallasites who had not been passed on and certified by the white oligarchy, or its arm in the black community, the ministerial alliance. But the trademark of the T.I. people entering city politics at this time was that they considered

156

themselves to be political "rationalists" who would not, in their own view of things, be "pushed" by threats or emotion. The initiative was always their own, and it was still for black people, as it had been before, to come forward politely and make requests, the difference being that this new white structure would listen occasionally.

These were a new breed of white people in Dallas, but they were, nevertheless, not entirely unlike the old breed. They had been attracted to the city in the first place, after all. They were corporate careerists, for the most part, relatively conservative themselves in the contexts they had left behind. They weren't former night riders, but they weren't hippies either. They were the beginning of the mix that is now characteristic of the city's white population.

Certainly Erik Jonsson would not be pushed by people he considered radicals. Nothing tried him more than to be lectured by someone like Fred Bell, chairman of the Dallas chapter of the Angela Davis Liberation Party. Jonsson's white friends said in later years that the impatience and anger Jonsson felt on these occasions finally soured him on what had been the otherwise pleasant task of being the city's mayor and steward.

The fact was that Jonsson's touchiness about being "pushed" by black people extended to all black people, whether they were radical or moderate, rich or poor. In 1968, when black middle-class homeowners from the Singing Hills neighborhood came to Jonsson and the council to beg them to stop sabotaging struggling black middle-class neighborhoods by jamming them full of cheap apartment buildings, the delegation dared to mention that the existence of black middle-class residential areas had been one of the big tickets the city had used to avoid riots earlier in the decade. Jonsson told them angrily: "We don't appreciate the implied power push of this type of presentation."

Not having had one, it was already too late to use the riot as leverage, and, not having had one, too late to claim power. The black middle class had taken its pay in the form of segregated black middle-class enclaves. Through the balance of the sixties, through the 1970s and to this day, the black middle class would pay the pound of flesh in lack of control over the zoning and development of its own territory. The new T.I. liberals in Dallas felt compassion for black people, but they were never afraid of them.

The point was, at the time, that black people all over America were lecturing white people. It was that moment in the nation's history when black people walked out of the smoke and fire of the cities and said, "Damn right we did it, and we'll do it again if you don't look at us and listen when we talk." For the first time, white people in those cities did listen, because they were scared to death, but more than that, because their hearts had been torn open. They looked into the cities and saw that the black ghettos were hell and that white people had made that hell and that the black people who were threatening them were human beings. An enormous emotional catharsis swept those cities.

In that process, black people developed a sense of historical identity that was not class-bound, that was forged instead on the anvil of late-20th-century, North American, antiblack white racism. That didn't happen in Dallas. What happened in Dallas was what had always happened before — a process of accommodation that did not achieve any change in anyone's fundamental vision of the world. While basic and fundamental change took place in the rest of the country, a smaller and more incremental evolution took place in Dallas, until finally Dallas was noticeably out of step. When the national Civil Rights Movement finally found its way to Dallas in the late 1960s, its first scouts felt as if they had fallen into a pocket in time.

"It was a real time warp," Peter Johnson remembers now. Johnson was still in his early 20s when he hit town in 1969, but he was by then a battle-hardened ranger in the civil rights wars raging back and forth across the South for a decade. Raised in the harshly segregated atmosphere of Plaquemine in Iberville Parish, Louisiana, where his father had been active in organizing the Voters League, Johnson spent his early teenage years messing around with kids in a hick town gang called the Trojans. By late teenage, he had talked the Trojans into turning their skills toward politics in the youth wing of the NAACP. By the late 1960s, he was one of the best of a generation of young organizers — smart, sophisticated by years of hard political struggle and travel, and trained. As soon as he got off the plane at Love Field in 1969 and started trying to deal with Dallas, he felt as if he were back somewhere in a past that even he didn't fully remember.

"Nobody would even rent us an office. In South Dallas! People here, black folks, didn't even understand a picket line. They'd walk right through it. There were white liberals, but they were so damned paternalistic you could not believe it. The Southern Christian Leadership Conference did a study of hunger in Dallas, and the liberal whites would say, 'Shucks, you know there's no hunger in Dallas. You're embarrassing us. Naturally you know there's no hungry people here.' "

The SCLC had sent Johnson to Dallas as part of a nationwide sweep to promote a movie it had produced on the life of the recently assassinated Dr. Martin Luther King. Johnson's orders were strict: "Get in, get the money, get out. The SCLC at the time was very concerned about not getting committed to things it didn't have the resources to handle. I was supposed to promote the movie, show it, send the money back to Atlanta and get out of town."

Johnson found that it wasn't going to be that simple. He found a situation in Dallas that troubled his conscience as a civil rights worker. He wound up staying in Dallas for several years.

"We had just never thought of Texas as being part of the South," he said. "From time to time, we would hear about things going on in Texas, but we were from the South, and we thought of the South as where the action was, where the need was."

At the same time, Dallas very clearly had not thought of itself as part of the South, either, at least not for purposes of participation in the civil rights upheaval of the period. When he first showed up in Dallas, Johnson was described by the local press as a "civil rights worker from the South." He remembers that conservative black leaders in Dallas "told me to go back to the South where I belonged."

When he arrived, Johnson was immediately struck by the realization that, in overlooking Dallas, the Civil Rights Movement had overlooked a great deal, indeed. Black people as well as white people talked about all the progress that had been made in Dallas, how the schools had been desegregated peacefully. Yet the schools were still completely segregated. Nothing could better have symbolized the gap between what people said about the schools and what was really true than the annual graduation ceremonies.

In the late 1960s, with a black man sitting on the school board, School Superintendent W. T. White still dared to hold racially segregated graduation ceremonies, a white ceremony and a "Negro" graduation ceremony. Some black leaders spoke out angrily. Kathlyn Gilliam, who would sit on the board one day herself, said in 1968: "We are sick and fed up with having more prejudice, hatred and jealousy on the board than love and compassion for all people. We are demanding the opportunity to study together in Dallas schools, and that the school system fully include the involvement of all. Stop asking what you can do for the Negro. You can't do anything for the Negro when you think of him as an inferior being."

159

However, most of the city's black leadership still was not speaking out in the same tones that were being heard in the rest of the country when Peter Johnson arrived. In fact, the main body of the traditional black leadership in the city, still centered on the old alliance of black ministers that the Citizens Council had always done business with. They sincerely believed black people had made great strides in Dallas — often citing the eminence of Zan Holmes — and that they should be satisfied with their lot. Johnson explains, "I had serious problems about coming in and taking resources out of the community without putting something back. When I first came to Dallas and wrote my first letter back to Atlanta, I said the black community here was 20 years behind the political development of blacks in Jackson, Mississippi."

29

In 1965, Mayor Jonsson established a framework of meetings and seminars for community leaders, many of them from far afield of the old Citizens Council ranks, which he called "Goals for Dallas." A year later, a series of articles by Dennis Hoover in The Dallas Morning News — a newspaper that was even then beginning to undergo gradual and healthy change — shocked many of the city's new high-tech residents. At a time when Americans everywhere had been stirred by the educational alarms being sounded by national education reformer Dr. James Conant, people in Dallas had special reason to be distressed.

Dallas was the largest city in the country that provided no kindergarten program at all; of the 10 biggest districts in Texas, it had the seventh worst teacher/pupil ratio; of the 12 biggest districts, it was 11th in the amount of school taxes collected; but of the 10 biggest districts in the state, Dallas had the biggest tax base.

Racism, not surprisingly, had much to do with the problems of the district. Superintendent White had encouraged a program by which the school system provided only minimal elements of the school setting — buildings and personnel for the most part — while parent groups provided all of the extras, encyclopedias and additional reading materials. That way, middle-class white people could spend money on their own schools and not have to subsidize poor whites or blacks.

Out of the Goals for Dallas activities, and spurred on by Dennis

Hoover's continuing work, a group of white people associated with
T.I., the medical science community, and other growing camps of
newcomers in the city began gathering around the schools issue. In
1965, the group descended on an organization that had just been
created by Don Fielding, one of the city's few real firebrand liberals.
They persuaded Fielding to step down as leader, and they reform-
ulated the group, called LEAD, around a racially moderate pro-
education platform.

In the next four years, LEAD mounted a successful raid on the
school board, throwing out several members who had been annointed
by the oligarchy and eventually helping to seat Dr. Emmett Conrad,
the first elected black member of the board in Dallas history. Conrad
needed the help: In order to get elected, he had to buck the resistance
of the Interdenominational Ministerial Alliance, which did not
believe blacks were ready yet for that sort of thing.

The relationship of LEAD and the black community, however, was
less than perfectly comfortable. Two years before Conrad ran, Dr.
Charles Hunter, a black sociologist at Bishop College, had sought
LEAD's endorsement and was refused. "They were willing to help,
but they didn't want to endorse me," Hunter remembers now. "The
reasoning of course was that this was the second year of LEAD, and
they didn't want to get 'typed' as a minority-oriented maybe radical-
type group. They were supposed to have been a group that valued
education, rather than politics."

Two years later, better organized and having made a strong showing
at the polls already, LEAD risked endorsing Conrad, but not without
a certain manipulative intent. Dr. Norman Kaplan, who was president of LEAD at the time, says now: "We never shied away from saying there has to be a good school system across the city, and we have
to spend the monies where the facilities are the least. But integration
was never our main interest. We were interested in schools. The
blacks were used mainly for their votes."

Kaplan is candid and straightforward about how it worked. The
black votes supporting LEAD candidates had not come from the old-
line black leadership, many of whom had been afraid of LEAD. Instead, the black people who worked with and for LEAD were of a new
emerging group of political activists centered in the Fair Park area. In
the late 1960s, toward the end of LEAD's brief existence, the new
black leaders from Fair Park came to the window to cash out.

"It was at a meeting in East Dallas, in Stanley Marcus' home,"

Kaplan said. "Two of them, Elsie Faye Heggins and J. B. Jackson, came and proposed Arthur Joe Fred, a black letter-carrier who wanted to run for the school board seat from the Fair Park area. Here was a black, coming to our committee saying, 'I want to represent my area,' and we had to say, 'Sorry, you're not qualified.' That caused a loss of willingness on their part to go along with us."

No great loss, however, since the whole operation was about to dissolve anyway. At the very end of the 1960s, when the busing orders began to come down and real integration looked briefly as if it might actually take place, LEAD's North Dallas/T.I.-high-tech/quasi-liberal support vanished. "They associated us with integration," Kaplan said. "We got creamed."

The whites yanked their kids, took off for the educational hills, and they haven't come back yet. Their brief experiment with biracial politics on the school board, however, left one thing behind: Elsie Faye Heggins.

People like J. B. Jackson and Elsie Faye Heggins were just coming into politics then because they more or less couldn't stay out. The traditional black leadership, led by S. M. Wright, head of the ministerial alliance, wasn't doing anything for them, and, meanwhile, the City of Dallas was off on another of its land grabs, using eminent domain to throw black families out of the area surrounding the state fairgrounds.

In public, of course, the line was that the fair — an increasingly deserted and desolate place during most of the year, as more and more of white Dallas moved north and away from it — had suddenly discovered it needed a whole lot of new parking area. The entire community of black people around the fairgrounds, unfortunately, would have to move. In private, that was not the story, and at least one published city report said brazenly that attendance at the fair had declined in recent years because fairgoers objected to being exposed to "a certain element" on their way into Fair Park.

In spite of the strict orders the SCLC had given him not to get gummed up in Dallas politics, Peter Johnson found himself drawn irresistibly to the Fair Park homeowners movement, in part because he couldn't believe how naive the black people were who were losing their homes. Cut off from the old-line black political structure, the main support they had been able to garner outside their own tiny community had come from a white liberal group called the Fair Park Block Partnership, associated with the University Park Methodist

163

Church and including some of the same people who were in LEAD.

"They were caught up in the old trick, where the liberals come to help them but then spend all their time telling them not to be confrontational and not to make trouble," Johnson said. "I couldn't believe how little they knew. They didn't even know about any of the Supreme Court decisions on eminent domain. We had been working on eminent domain matters in, SCLC and in the Civil Rights Movement everywhere in the South. For years! I said, listen, we got a bunch of lawyers in Atlanta we can bring in here and at least get you some help."

Elsie Faye Heggins went on to become the first black city council member elected from a single-member district in Dallas history. She owed the white establishment nothing, and she reminded them of it often. She refused to do any of the shuffling, smiling, and soft-speaking that the oligarchy still considered de rigueur of blacks in the late 1970s. She drove the old Citizens Council crowd absolutely mad, and many black people in Dallas loved her for it. But 20 years ago, when Peter Johnson found her and her mentor, J. B. Jackson, trying to figure things out in the Fair Park homeowners movement, they were unlikely firebrands.

"Elsie Faye and Jackson were not aware of their blackness. They were property-owners. They were independent, but they hadn't gotten into blackness at all."

While he became involved in issues in Dallas, Johnson and the SCLC saw to it that some of the black activists emerging from the Fair Park struggle were sent to training workshops, where they were introduced to theoretical politics and to some of the history of the Civil Rights Movement. Meanwhile, Johnson was doing what he could to teach by example.

In the summer of 1969, the traditional black leadership had become exasperated by the refusal of the people who owned little frame houses around Fair Park to take the money the city had offered them. City Councilman George Allen, a black man who had been placed on the city council by the white oligarchy as its contribution to the sixties, had been given the job of talking sense into the Fair Park homeowners, but he came away from what was to have been his last meeting with them having decided they were under some sort of spell.

"The people there basically were not the homeowners involved," Allen said. "They were SNNC people and black militants. The black people present were completely subdued by the rhetoric of these other people."

Mrs. Miriam Schult of University Park, one of the block partners, was concerned, too. She was worried that any picketing the group might do could be exploited by "outside groups" trying to "do their own thing." And John Perricone, black middle-class co-chairman of the partnership, insisted that the issue had entirely and only to do with money and was "not a black cause."

The cause, of course, was entirely a black cause, and the issue was completely racial. The black people who lived around Fair Park were living incarnations of everything that had happened to blacks in Dallas since the 1930s. Gidding Johnson, 66, was the archetypical Fair Park homeowner. He had bought his home for $8,000 in 1952, just after the special grand jury had bluffed out an end to the bombings in South Dallas. He and his wife were the first black people in the area. Before moving to the Fair Park area, they had lived in rented rooms since coming to Dallas from Bryan, Texas in 1923.

Owning a house had been unthinkable. They both worked as domestics. Then, at the height of the recruitment drives for World War II, the enlistment age was raised to 45, and Gidding Johnson signed up. Four years later, he returned to Dallas and to his wife with $300 in mustering out pay. She had good news: She had saved $200 during his absence. Together, they had enough money to make a down payment on a house — to become homeowners.

"She put all she earned into this house," he said in the summer of 1969. "She was happy here, but she died in 1958."

Eventually, Johnson paid the house off. He painted it avocado green. The lot was 50 feet by 150 feet. He filled most of the area around the house with flowers. "It does me good to see things grow," he said. "I've always wanted them, and now I have them."

This was the unpleasant "element" the city wanted to spare fairgoers from seeing on their way into the hallowed Fair Park. Semi-retired, bent, peering through thick glasses, still working part time as a school crossing-guard and part time as a butler and waiter, Gidding Johnson didn't want to move, and he was heartsick that the city would give him only $8,700 for his property — less than half what it would cost to buy another house at the time. Bruce Hunter, chief right-of-way agent for the city, expressed sympathy. "There's no doubt he has taken care of his place. It looks nice. It's a real credit to the neighborhood." But Hunter explained, ". . . we have to make our offer strictly on value and not on how the improvements are kept up."

Strictly business. The properties just weren't worth that much, what with 161 empty houses in the area, 101 demolished lots and a serious rat problem. That's how eminent domain works. That's how it had worked around Love Field, in Little Egypt, Eagle Ford, all over town, for a long, long time.

30

George Allen was certainly right in his sense that the Fair Park homeowners had come under a new sort of spell, and the white liberals of the Block Partnership were correct in believing that Fair Park was slipping from their control, too. But no one saw what Fair Park really was. It was the beginning of the end for the entire system in Dallas, for the racial system, for the political system, for the oligarchy itself. Finally here, on the soil surrounding the ritual center of the kingdom of R. L. Thornton, a new fire was to be lit against the dark.

Peter Johnson was working hard and fast to show the homeowners where to find sources of power that were unfettered by connections to the white power structure and, what may have been tougher, to develop their own power free of obligations to the Interdenominational Ministerial Alliance and the rest of the old black power structure. Johnson made sure that black people in Dallas would hear what major figures in the Civil Rights Movement believed about all this talk of Dallas as a model of modern race relations. He brought a very young Jesse Jackson to town, and Jackson read the law to everyone who came to hear him speak at Warren United Methodist Church on Oakland Avenue.

"Dallas is a wicked city," Jackson thundered. "I saw the downtown skyscrapers, and I saw the great buildings built by fortunes that came out of oil exploration . . . but I have seen in H. L. Hunt's town white people starving."

He pledged "war" to bring economic welfare to the black people of Dallas. But Jackson told his listeners one major and significant untruth. He promised them the national Civil Rights Movement, having discovered the plight of black people in Dallas, had come to stay: "We ain't just passing through town," Jackson said. "We ain't camping in Dallas. We're gonna live here for a while."

As for the George Allens and the S. M. Wrights of the world, the Fair Park homeowner movement was to be their Waterloo, although it would be many years before they recognized the real dimension of the political defeat they had suffered there. For one thing, Peter Johnson and the SCLC started saying things about the traditional black leadership that had never been said before in public. Willie Bolden of the SCLC national staff came to Dallas to help carry out a study of hunger in the city and quickly became involved with Johnson in Fair Park.

Both Johnson and Bolden were amazed at first, and then furious when they realized that some leaders in the Interdenominational Ministerial Alliance were working against them in their efforts to show the movie chronicling the life of the martyred Martin Luther King. During his life, King's relationship with the black clergy of Dallas had been tenuous at best. The Dallas clergy had shunned him during his early visits to the city and had only reluctantly come around to deal with him after their own parishioners had been swept ahead of them into the vast reverence most black people of the period felt for King.

White conservative feeling against King had been especially harsh in Texas. Governor John Connally had shocked much of the rest of the nation the day after King was murdered by suggesting, in the process of issuing an official condolence, that King had probably helped bring his own death upon himself. "He contributed much to the chaos and the strife and the confusion and the uncertainty in this country," Connally said, "but, whatever his actions, he deserved not the fate of assassination."

That was just Texas talking. That was nothing new. After all, it had been the squabble over Connally's resistance to the civil rights legislation championed by the Kennedys, in part, that had brought JFK to Dallas, and to his death.

What was inconceivable to the SCLC people, in the wake of King's recent and still deeply embittering murder, was that any black leader in Dallas, any black leader in the world for that matter, could dishonor him by working against a showing of the film biography. In their anger, the SCLC began to say things to black Dallasites about their traditional leaders that worried the traditional leaders very much.

Bolden lashed out during a speech at Faith Cumberland Presbyterian Church, accusing Rev. S. M. Wright of using his position as head of the ministerial alliance to do everything possible to "keep us black folks quiet for his white friends."

Some black leaders from within the city responded by sounding similar notes. Dr. Charles Hunter, the Bishop College sociologist, sneered at the vaunted racial progress of the city, telling Dallas black people what the poor ones already knew: that the comfort of black people in the Hamilton Park and Singing Hills neighborhoods of the city had been bought at the expense of poor blacks.

"In income, the change is at the top," Hunter said. "At the bottom, it has become worse."

It was for Peter Johnson to demonstrate the difference, to act it out, to show the black people who were being thrown out of their homes around Fair Park where power really comes from. Consistently, from the very beginning, Mayor Jonsson had refused to meet with the homeowners.

Their plight was, he said, a business matter between them and the city manager. It would be wrong, it would not be rational, it would not be the Dallas way at all for Erik Jonsson to interfere or become involved in the process in any way. His pride in this matter was personal and separate from even the rest of the city council, who did meet with the neighborhood in June of 1969. At that time, Jonsson had refused to attend the meeting, because, he said, he couldn't run down to every little neighborhood in town every time someone had a problem and "have a meeting in their living room." He might have been part of the new breed, but he still had to think of Dallas as a whole.

Peter Johnson told the homeowners that they ought to make the mayor meet with them, in their homes, in his office if necessary, but they should force him to meet them. They asked why, what good it would do, how could the mayor change anything since the meeting with the rest of the council hadn't done any good. He told them they needed to do it on principle, because they were citizens of the city and were losing their homes, and the mayor of the city ought to look them in the face and listen to them and speak to them, whether it did any good or not.

Most of the homeowners thought, no matter what principle was involved, that Peter Johnson was crazy and that the mayor never would do it. The mayor was a millionaire, a white prince of the city, a pillar and a stalwart of the oligarchy no matter what else he may have been, and he would never come down to a black neighborhood to talk to a bunch of butlers and maids, especially if those butlers and maids gave him the impression that they were even thinking of "pushing." That was just how it was in Dallas, how it always had been. That was especially how it was with Mr. Erik Jonsson. Dallas was an ordered city. Everything had its order and the order needed to be respected. Even the white people only got ahead by respecting the order, by working their ways up slowly through the labyrinth of committees and commissions, charities and volunteer activities until the men at the top finally smiled upon them. So had the black community been given its order, its system of rank and caste, centered on the ministerial alliance and, through the ministerial alliance, drawing its power from the Citizens Council, from the oligarchy itself. Demanding that the mayor stoop to meet with black servants, that he bend to their will, was demanding that the entire logic of the city turn itself inside out.

Peter Johnson laughed. He told them they were worried about something that simply was not a problem: All the mayor needed was a proper invitation. On December 30, 1969, 48 hours before the first nationally televised playing of the Cotton Bowl football game was to be aired from the sacred fairgrounds in Dallas, Peter Johnson sent the mayor his invitation: Johnson informed the mayor that 600 marchers would stop the Cotton Bowl Parade on national television on New Year's Day if, by then, the mayor had not conducted a meeting with the Fair Park homeowners to discuss their grievances. The mayor had until midnight on the night of Dec. 31 to meet with the homeowners. If no meeting had occurred by then, the homeowners would take a position on the parade route and occupy it until removed by force.

Johnson told the mayor in his note that one of the networks would be in town and had been notified and that all of the local media had been similarly alerted. When the local press asked Johnson how he could attempt such a demonstration when, according to the police, he had acquired no parade permit for his group, Johnson said: "We've been told that what we're doing is against the law, and I think it's kind of silly to get a permit to break the law."

It was a grim New Year's Eve for Erik Jonsson. On that night, the

Reverend Mark Herbener, a white Lutheran pastor whose Mt. Olive Lutheran Church is in the heart of the black community on what is now Martin Luther King Boulevard, had turned his church's basement over to the Fair Park homeowners and their supporters, many of whom were white.

"It was really moving to watch the process affect some of these North Dallas block partnership people," Johnson says now. "They started out with all of their condescending liberal attitudes, and then, when they saw what was going on, when they saw that the city was giving black people one price for their property and a white property owner right next to them three times that amount, they said, 'Hey, that's not right. That's terrible!' And they became radicalized."

Almost 500 people were huddled in the church basement, prepared to leave the basement at midnight and march to the processional route of the Cotton Bowl parade, where they would take a stand. Peter Johnson had figured out the ceremonial workings of the city brilliantly. Whatever else might happen in Dallas, whatever the strictures might be against nonhierarchical dialogue, the oligarchy could not and would not allow a desecration of the Cotton Bowl Parade. Certainly not with the whole world watching.

For his part, Johnson had no intention of going through with trying to stop the parade, but, of course, only he knew that at the time. "I had a contingency plan to get out of it if the city didn't buckle, because it would have been a bloodbath, and we didn't send old people and supporters and people like that out to get their heads busted. But I didn't tell anybody in the church that night I was bluffing, and I made damn sure they (the Citizens Council) didn't know I was bluffing."

Repeated bomb threats were called in to the church. Johnson says the threats did not necessarily come from the white hierarchy. They were not the ones most immediately threatened by what was going on that night in the basement of Mt. Olive Lutheran. "The black ministers were the ones who had the most to lose. If we could reach around them and make things happen in the white power structure, then they would no longer be needed. They would lose their power base."

At various points in the evening, the group was canvassed to see who desired or needed to leave. At one point, there was actually a drill in which people who were willing to go to jail were arrayed on one side of the room and checked to ensure they were armed with toothbrushes. Through the evening, calls and then emissaries came to invite Peter Johnson to meet with this official at City Hall or that one and finally to come and meet with Mayor Jonsson.

"I said hell no. What do I want to meet with Erik Jonsson for? I'm not losing my home. These are the people he needs to meet with."

Finally, late that night, not long before the deadline, word came that the mayor would meet with the Fair Park homeowners in his office. Peter Johnson rode with a delegation of the homeowners that included J. B. Jackson, but he parted company with them in the corridor outside the mayor's office. The homeowners went in and talked to the mayor by themselves.

There are two ends to the story. One is that they all lost their homes. They got more money for their property than the city had been offering before the Cotton Bowl ploy, but they all lost their homes. Some of the land on which their neighborhood stood has been used by now for parking, but most of it is barren rutted dirt — a grotesque monument to white Dallas' contempt for black property rights and for law.

But there is another and infinitely more important end to the Cotton Bowl story. Real estate and buildings, dirt and mortar are meaningless and trivial against the power of ideas and the incredible magic of images. When they headed into their meeting with Erik Jonsson, the Fair Park homeowners remembered Peter Johnson's one stern admonition — that they not come out of the meeting without a symbol.

The next day, when the people of South Dallas stepped back out of their own streets to make the customary safe passage for the Cotton Bowl Parade — rolling down out of the city, with its army of high-stepping white girls in pink paramilitary uniforms and proud white college boys on tissue-paper floats — they saw that the parade was led, as usual, by a single Cadillac convertible. In the convertible sat Mayor Erik Jonsson. And J. B. Jackson.

"They stood there," Peter Johnson remembers, "and they looked . . . and they said . . . WOW!"

Riding into the ritual center of the city, sharing the carriage of the mayor himself, was J. B. Jackson, a Fair Park homeowner, who was there not because he had earned the favor of the ministers who had earned the favor of the white men who had earned the favor of the oligarchy, but because he had threatened to stop the parade. In Dallas, that was one of those moments like the moment when Rosa Parks decided not to go to the back of the bus in Montgomery, when, in

Cleaver's words, the gears moved in the universe.

Out of the Fair Park homeowner movement came the first black leaders in Dallas who seized power without permission from the white community, who understood that power had to be seized, and could never be received as a gift or token. The Fair Park homeowners became the plaintiffs in the federal suit that finally brought down the old at-large election system, depriving the oligarchy of its principal mechanism of political control.

It was not until the end of the 1970s that federal court orders abolishing the system gave the new black political leadership real access to the reins at City Hall. The first truly independent candidate to take office under that new regime was Elsie Faye Heggins, an alumna of the Fair Park homeowner movement. She had been seasoned by then in long battles over the creation of the Martin Luther King community center in South Dallas and in the fights over the administration of War on Poverty programs. However, it was not until 1980 that the white community at large began to see her on the news every Wednesday evening after the weekly council meeting.

For all the excitement she aroused in white North Dallas, Mrs. Heggins was an unlikely terrorist. In the fight over the War on Poverty, she had alarmed all of white Dallas and had gotten everyone all battened down and prepared for a bloody uprising when she used the "mother" word in a shouted exchange with then-Mayor Wes Wise, who subsequently became a friend and supporter. Once she was elected to the city council, her manner became almost demure by most people's standards for fed-up angry black people in America. She wore her hair straightened and dressed and behaved like a quiet church lady for the most part. When she talked back to new Mayor Robert Folsom, she did so with eyes cast down and voice raised and just barely trembling. But she talked back. She told the mayor and the white members of the council that they were racists. She didn't laugh when they laughed. She didn't want them to like her. She didn't like them.

When Mrs. Heggins was giving him the business, the body language of Mayor Folsom was worth a million words. Accustomed to black people who spoke in answers, not questions, and never ever in accusations, the former SMU footballer and millionaire apartment developer took even the most timorously expressed opposition from Mrs. Heggins as if it were a savage body blow. Most but not all of the time, Folsom managed to not shout and waggle a parental finger at

Mrs. Heggins, but he seemed to suffer excruciating physical pain whenever she spoke to him, twisting and writhing in his seat, holding his head and grimacing. At every Wednesday council meeting, Heggins and Folsom reenacted this danse macabre again for the television cameras, and every Wednesday evening on the 6 o'clock news it played to raves in the black community, each of the mayor's grimaces earning Mrs. Heggins another heartfelt wave of uncritical devotion from her followers.

The larger Civil Rights Movement, meanwhile, had not stayed around as long as Jesse Jackson had promised. The Dallas Fair Park homeowner movement was one of its last classic organizing efforts, before a long and dispiriting passage in which the SCLC spent most of its time on economic boycotts and drifted away from the fundamental moral issues of Martin Luther King, finally losing its momentum over questions of money and ethics. Peter Johnson was called back to Atlanta in the early 1970s and eventually drifted out of the SCLC and out of the movement.

31

When Comer Cottrell showed up in Dallas in 1981, his arrival was the occasion for consternation and pain in the traditional leadership of the black community. As soon as Cottrell stepped off the plane, he was placed on the Citizens Council, the first black member in its history, and on the executive committee of the Dallas Chamber of Commerce and on the boards of directors of influential banks and companies in Dallas. That kind of access is still almost totally unheard of in the Dallas black community, where black businessmen are proud to serve on the separate Black Chamber of Commerce, formerly the Negro Chamber of Commerce, and where almost none of the major corporations or banks have black members on their boards.

Cottrell brought with him Proline, a $23-million-a-year cosmetics company he founded in Los Angeles and still owns, along with some stout political connections. But more important, he brought with him a certain attitude. He was already playing the game the same way the white boys played it in Dallas. He was good at it, and he left Los Angeles and brought his company to Dallas for the same reasons white CEOs bring their companies to Dallas — because it is a businessman's town, where they play the game the businessman's way.

"I love it," he said four years after coming to Dallas. Sitting at a small tea table at one end of his enormous office in the new plant he has built on the levee in Oak Cliff, overlooking downtown, he said, "I just love this place, because Dallas is still run by entrepreneurs. I think just like those boys downtown.

"If business is evil," he said, "Dallas is evil. I think business is wonderful. If Dallas is ruthless, sometimes you have to be ruthless. My decision to come was based entirely on the business environment. This is the kind of town I like. Love. I love Dallas. If I say anything negative about Dallas, it's because I'm hoping to help it change for the better."

Like many blacks who have come to Dallas from other places over the last decade, Cottrell's criticisms are aimed more often at black Dallas than at white Dallas. It's his thesis that white people everywhere behave like white people, but that the white people in Dallas at least respect money and strength, and black people in Dallas should have figured that out by now. His problem with black people in Dallas is that he thinks they still play by separate and more ginger rules. For their part, the older black leaders in Dallas have been deeply suspicious of Cottrell, especially of his connections with the Republican Party.

When he first came to Dallas, Cottrell bought a mansion in Oak Cliff, where most of the city's wealthy black families live, but after two years he moved to North Dallas, where the white money lives.

"The white community helped me," Cottrell said. "The black community told me to go to hell. I got tired of inviting people over to my house in Oak Cliff and never getting invited back. Because of the fast track I came in on, I was an unknown entity. Why was I being accepted, and they had been here so long, doing right, and they had not been?"

It is there, at that point, that Cottrell finds fault with the traditional black leadership in Dallas, for not realizing that the white money in Dallas didn't put Comer Cottrell on any boards because people thought he had good manners; they put him on the boards, he says, for two reasons: 1) because he had enough money and power to do some good for the city, and 2) because he had enough money and power to do some harm. The ultimate proof that black people in Dallas have been more harmed than helped by the hovering attentions of the white power structure, he argues, is that the white power structure now has no respect for them.

"Black people here don't understand that there's no reason to have blacks on corporate boards here, because blacks here don't understand how blacks got on the boards elsewhere. They weren't put on those boards because they were liked. They were put on by pressure and through the threat of boycott."

Cottrell is a successful, smart businessman who operates close to the very heart of power in Dallas after only a few years in town, hand in glove with the white power structure, and yet, in spite of all that, he is one of many black power figures in Dallas who wonder openly and sincerely whether the absence of a riot in Dallas' history has been an entirely good thing.

"In Dallas, that power is never able to come together. Blacks are so segmented. It was good that they didn't have a riot here, because they didn't have to live with the scars, but, by the same token, it did not pull the community together with a common interest.

"In Atlanta and Birmingham and L.A., the class structure fell during that period because we all were the same, unified by our blackness, so we had a common agenda for then."

Cottrell thinks that, eventually, Dallas will be a good city for blacks because it will provide them with the only thing that counts — opportunity in an atmosphere of free-wheeling upbeat free enterprise. The difficulty Cottrell encounters in preaching that sermon is that he is often misunderstood as proposing that black people be more accommodating in their approach to white business. He says he is preaching the opposite — that black people take on white money by the shirt-front and shake it until something falls out, that they be as aggressive in business, in other words, as the white boys are, and that they do everything they can to make themselves independent. With money.

"I know exactly who I am. My money comes 100 percent from black people, here in Dallas, in Southern California, in Africa, all over the world, from black people, so I'm free from white intimidation."

When he looks into the local black community to see who might come close to understanding what he's saying, he doesn't mention the well-educated black people who came out of Hamilton Park and Singing Hills. He thinks of people who stood up and told off the white community. People from Fair Park.

"I think Mrs. Heggins was good in her term for the city, even though she was not diplomatic," he said, "even though she was not intellectual. She was the catalyst for a lot of things that have happened in the city. Even though she wasn't liked, she was effective."

Of course, Comer Cottrell is the head of his own large company and can afford to deal with Dallas in the broad swashbuckling style the city appreciates. Most human beings have to fend at a somewhat more mundane level of existence, and there, at the level of the worker, there is perhaps even more discomfort between black people from elsewhere and black people who grew up in Dallas.

Paula Walker, a black television executive who came to Dallas several years ago by way of Harlem and Vassar, says white people and black people went through a lot of mutual conditioning elsewhere during the 1960s that just didn't get done in Dallas. White people in Dallas, for example, don't know what's funny and what's enough to get your lights punched out. She tells a story about a trip her former husband made back to the North with a group of fellow insurance inspectors, whose firm in Connecticut had called them back for training. Ahead of him on the plane, two white colleagues were raucously teasing a black colleague.

"My husband said that, all the way up there on the plane, these two white guys from Dallas kept kidding the black man from Dallas about how much they could get for him if they sold him back into slavery, auctioned him off when they got off the plane or something, and the black man kept laughing and going along with it. Finally, when they started to descend, my husband walked up to them, and he said to the white guys: 'You're in the North now, you're not back in Dallas, so you need to cut that shit out right now if you don't want to get your asses kicked.' And he turned to the black guy and said, 'As for you, you really need to get your shit together in a hurry and don't let people talk to you that way. We keep our white boys better trained than that up here.' "

When Peter Johnson returned to Dallas in the 1980s, he was no longer a civil rights worker. He was a middle-class father and construction contractor approaching middle age who had come back to Dallas for the same reasons everyone else was coming — because the city's buoyant and seemingly impregnable economy offered promise, because it was a place where he could reasonably hope to make some money, make some personal progress, get and have some of what he hadn't been able to get where he had been before. At a time when much of the rest of the nation was in economic decline, Dallas was the rising wave. But after he had returned and settled his own camp enough to have time to look around, Peter Johnson felt that old familiar sense of the Dallas time warp. At a time when his old confrere of the Civil Rights Movement, Andy Young, was running Atlanta, when another member of the Young clan, Coleman Young, was sitting down with the leaders of the auto industry to determine the future of Detroit and Michigan, when black mayors and congressmen all over the country were pulling open doors black people hadn't even known existed 20 years ago, Dallas still seemed somehow mired in the 1960s. The Fair Park homeowners, much as he understood and loved them, seemed barely closer to the outer ring than they had been when he had left them in 1973.

"The Elsie Faye Hegginses and the J. B. Jacksons have never moved beyond those times," Johnson says now. "All they saw then, every day, all they knew was SCLC propaganda. They saw things happen through confrontation that were productive. But they've never grown out of that. They're still only related to poor people issues. They're unable to relate to the overall community. They're aloof from the black middle class."

Far from believing what the Heggins-Jackson wing of the black community in Dallas does today is wrong, he just doesn't think it does enough or that the larger black community in Dallas has moved ahead enough, and he blames both Dallas and the Civil Rights Movement of the 1960s for the fact that the few assertive leaders in the black community in Dallas today are so isolated.

Looking back on those years from the vantage of the 1980s, Johnson feels again, as he felt when he first came in 1969, that the Civil Rights Movement gave Dallas short shrift. "The SCLC never took Dallas seriously. We never had the commitment to this part of the country that we did to other parts of the country."

What the movement did manage to accomplish in Dallas he thinks was fairly shallow. "Sure, we could come in and provide leadership, but that doesn't provide local leadership or a sense of peoplehood."

Johnson's assessment of race relations in Dallas today is harsh. Black people in Dallas today, he says, pay a dear price for never having shown real resistance. "There is no respect for the black community here, because the black community has never given the power structure reason to respect it."

He sees no sense of unity in the black community in Dallas, and, for that, Johnson blames the historical absence in Dallas of a real struggle. "When a community collectively has to confront its oppressor, the traditional things lose their meaning. The oppressor, confronted, will beat the doctor in the head just as soon as he would beat me in the head, and, all of a sudden, the doctor who still isn't sure if he wanted to become a Negro becomes a black doctor. Crisis creates a sense of peoplehood that didn't exist before.

"Everywhere I worked in the movement before I came to Dallas, there came a point when you could look in the eyes of people and see a change in their sense of commitment and who they were. Whenever there was a struggle and people took command of their own fate, a certain look came into their eyes. You could see in their eyes whether they had done it yet or not. When they stopped being Negroes and became black people, their eyes came up level and they looked at the world differently. I have never seen that look in Dallas. To this day, I have not seen it."

What should really give pause to the old-style white leadership in Dallas is that even people at the reasonable center of the black political spectrum in Dallas worry that racial peace, while worthy in most obvious respects, may have been in other ways a Trojan horse, bringing into the city certain liabilities that may only now be coming into full operation. The Reverend Zan Holmes rejoices that there was no riot, but he says in the next breath that there was a negative side, too: "I think that in some ways the city suffered, because a lot of emotion and anger that was present among oppressed peoples was frustrated and was never openly expressed so the community at large could see it. Because it was real. It was there, believe me.

"In many instances, black folks took their anger out on each other, as in the warring of the militants and the conservatives in the black community. What was happening was that the powers that be were on top of this potentially explosive situation, always able to move very quickly and when necessary to give up something. Maybe not much, but just enough.

"Many people in Dallas assumed Dallas was better off than it really was. Although I don't like violence and would never call for it, the fact remains that the powder keg was smoldering during those days. All the seeds of violence were here. I still think Dallas is a city that underestimates the anger poor folks feel."

The white business establishment's judgment of the traditional black community in Dallas now is even more pejorative than the opinions of black newcomers, but the bases for white criticism — and this is a key difference — are precisely the opposite of what people like Comer Cottrell are saying. Cottrell may be able to see that what white businessmen in Dallas really respect is money and guts, but the white business establishment does not see that in itself, at least not where the black community is concerned. The people who speak for the old oligarchy speak critically and even bitterly against the emerging black political leaders, especially the Fair Park crowd, because they blame them for having spoiled what was obviously a very good deal for the oligarchy. They are especially bitter over what may have been Peter Johnson's single greatest legacy — the destruction of the at-large system of electing local officials.

The at-large system had been the mechanical centerpiece of the old Citizens Council machine. With its money and its command over the obedient white majority, the Citizens Council had been able to dominate absolutely the formulation of slates for Dallas city offices and North Dallas state and county seats. The local Democratic Party, whose "liberal" wing was the one not in favor of a return to slavery, dominated the creation of slates for state and county offices in the unaffluent half of the county. The only way for anyone to get elected to anything in Dallas was to win the approval of either the Citizens Council machine or the Democratic Party machine.

Neither the Citizens Council nor the Democratic Party had illusions about the importance of the at-large system to the survival of the machinery in Dallas. Prodded by the LEAD education reform movement and the T.I. crowd, the local Democratic Party suffered Zan Holmes to serve in the Texas House of Representatives from 1968 to 1972, but the stalwarts of the party made it plain to Holmes that he was to keep his hands strictly out of, off, and away from anything to do with trying to change the at-large system through legislation.

"When I went to Austin, my Democratic colleagues from Dallas said, "You can vote any way you want except on single-member districts," Holmes says now. "That was the prize, the issue, the vote that mattered the most. Don't mess around with our single-member districts."

When the issue came up, Holmes disobeyed the Dallas delegation and voted in favor of single-member districts.

"That's where I incurred the most wrath of my career down there. That was the first time I ever got cussed out and called a nigger on the floor of the House, by the chairman of the Dallas delegation."

The attempts to destroy the at-large machinery with legislation failed, and it was Peter Johnson who encouraged the Fair Park homeowners to take the question to the federal courts. Eventually, the courts ruled that the at-large system was racially discriminatory. A new mixed system of single-member districts with just enough at-large districts to ensure continued white domination was put into effect in the mid-1970s and produced its first city council in 1978.

Alex Bickley of the Citizens Council sees the entire new order as a dark and foreboding chapter for the city, beginning with the creation of single-member districts. He says the business community fought so long and so hard against the creation of single-member districts because people in the old power structure believed single-member districts would ruin the very machinery that had brought Dallas its success.

"I think where the business community was coming from at the time was a comparison of Dallas with these cities that did have single-member districts. We stood so far above them, you wonder, 'Why substitute success for something else? We had seen what had happened in other cities. We had seen the Chicagos, the New Yorks, and Clevelands.

"True, you had a different type of representation (under the at-large system). You had the minority representative at the time, but the old argument is, 'Well, but we want to select our own.' The question comes in, what is most effective?

"Mrs. Heggins, she didn't take anything home to 'em. If you can't even get a motion seconded, your effectiveness isn't much. In that respect, she was a loser.

"It's a frustration. It's kind of like a fellow who files a lawsuit just based on principle. You can spend a lot of time and money and effort, and you end up with nothing.

"I think there is an earnest desire on the part of the business community to help the minority community in a real solid way. They are somewhat frustrated also in knowing how to do it, because of the different cultures and the different perspectives. They are doing some very definite and solid things.

"Not all of them are working, and they won't tomorrow or the next day, but there is a very dedicated and earnest attempt to help. It's kind of like an alcoholic. You can't help the individual that doesn't want to be helped."

There is real concern in the business establishment about whether the single-member system in particular and representative constituent-driven pluralistic politics in general will be able to coexist with the city manager system. Dallas has always taken enormous pride in being the largest city manager system in the nation. The city manager system has been a special rubric in the Dallas book of municipal faith, showing that Dallas runs like a business, like a company or corporation, which the Dallas establishment takes to be the highest evolution of human social order.

The single-member system, when it came into effect, was a new experience for the power-wielders of the city. In 1979, when the system was still brand new, a city council member who was a carryover from the old system told a reporter: "You don't have any idea what's going on down here. These people in my district are going crazy. They're calling me and trying to tell me that if I don't do what they say on these damned street projects, they'll vote against me and throw me out of office. And from what I've been told, they can do it!"

Indeed, and in fact, the destruction of the old slate system ripped a hole in the fabric of the oligarchical raiment that only widens with time, and there are thoughtful and involved people in Dallas who have real qualms about the long-range effects. George Schrader, now a typical and successful downtown Dallas entrepreneur/developer/lobbyist/businessman, was city manager of Dallas during the changeover to single-member districts. Schrader feels strongly that constituency politicians make a poor political support mechanism for a truly professional city manager system. The old notion, after all, was that the council would act as a kind of arms-length board of directors, handing down broad policy, leaving the city manager free to devote himself to implementation.

With considerable evidence to support him, Schrader argues that the Dallas City Council ceased being very good at coming up with policy after it started having to worry so much about getting reelected. The sudden dearth of policy directives from the council, Schrader says, meant that the city manager, in order to plan, had to come up with his own policies, and that has created real problems of legitimacy and credibility for the city manager system in Dallas. It also kept Schrader's hands full servicing constituent problems for the council members when he was city manager.

"It made adversaries between members of the council, fed conflict, and made members of the council provincial," Schrader said. "I told my staff, if you're going to have a water supply, I'm so caught up in catching dogs and putting in stop signs and meeting with people, it's important that someone do the planning, and you've got to do that, department heads."

As soon as the city manager and his staff began to reach across the line into policy, they became vulnerable to some good old-fashioned American skepticism, since, after all, it is not customary in this society for people to make public policy decisions without the benefit of an elective mandate — the only commonly recognized source of political legitimacy in most of the country. In the continued absence of a clear policy substrate from the council, the city manager system in Dallas continues to operate on borrowed political time, waiting for the single-member system to mature and catch up with its responsibilities.

Schrader believes, however, that the system will work against minorities when the majority finally learns how to work it. The minorities were better off, in his view, when the oligarchy was able to use the slate system to protect them.

"What's going to happen is that single-member districts are going to turn around and bite the minorities. They've lost the big ballgame. This is a prejudicial competitive system. People haven't learned how to use single-member districts yet. It will take another generation. When they do, they'll use it for some very unwholesome kinds of things. The lines will be drawn.

"We're in this cycle. This generation of leadership is driven by cause. They're not experienced or inclined toward compromise, and government is a compromise."

The black newcomers to Dallas, then, don't understand why the local black community is not more bold and independent, and the old white oligarchy is still bitter over the amount of independence the local black community has managed to attain. The black community in Dallas winds up with few champions. Among neither the new black critics nor the old white critics is there any decent understanding of the position that either black people in Dallas or the city itself have occupied in relation to the national culture in the last 30 years. Few people seem to recognize what sort of island, what kind of utter political isolation and eccentricity have been the condition of local life until very recently. In politics anyway, Dallas was annexed and became an integral part of the United States in 1978. Up to that moment, it was a well-run predemocratic city-state, ruled by a board of elders who valued wealth and ritual over truth and law.

32

There were bombings, terror, and injustice in other cities all over the country. There continue to be. Those were not what made Dallas unique. What was unique was the way the body of the city embraced and dealt with those problems. Events and persons and the flow of time conspired in Dallas to formulate a most untypical solution. Where the process was messy, often explosive and ragtag in other cities, it was neat, corporate, carefully managed, and efficiently repressive in Dallas. The black community in Dallas found itself caught in the compulsive grip of a white community struggling for self-control, of white people beset by demons of their own making.

The terror of the bombings of the early fifties was real and arresting, but worse was the slow and numbing effect of the aftermath, in which the white power structure publicly conceded that it could not or would not bring law to bear and would substitute instead its own authority, its own fiat. In one hand the power structure held the bear-leash and in the other a crust of bread.

Since there was not to be an independent appeal to law, the black community was totally dependent on the oligarchy to continue holding onto the leash and delivering the crust. Employment was steady, if not well paid, and the peace was being maintained; the black community in Dallas was in great shape, as long as the oligarchy didn't change its mind. That, of course, is why most people in our society prefer law to compassion, so they can close both eyes when they go to bed at night.

That did not happen in Dallas. The people who organized the bombings and arson attacks of the 1940s, 1950s and 1960s are still at large, comfortable and very much at peace, too, in the city, sitting on lawn chairs on just the other side of the fence, watching people come and go.

There was unresolved violence in other cities, too. But of course in many of those places the accrued violence of years of injustice really was requited, finally, in rioting. That did not happen in Dallas, and the reasons why it did not happen did not have to do entirely with jack-boot repression. A good deal of the urgency for peace that the levee boys felt in the early 1950s was founded on enormous optimism for the city; they looked out and saw the Emerald City rising up off the riverbottom, and they didn't want anything to happen to spoil their dream. In remarkable degree, their dream has come true, and it is their dream, realized, that draws people like Comer Cottrell to Dallas.

In the dream of the old white oligarchy, Comer Cottrell sees the dream of blacks, too — to be absolutely free, to have full dignity and full enfranchisement, to receive good educations, to make tons of money, wield power, have fun, to have everything that white people have.

Dallas has not begun to come full-face into confrontation with the political shame of the period before John F. Kennedy's assassination. Dallas has not yet conceded that Dallas did kill Kennedy, by fostering intolerance and by depriving ordinary citizens of the most important source of sanity in American society — political self-determination. The fact is that the enormous urgency produced by the backlash after the assassination reinvigorated the city's will to find its way to racial peace. At a time when Detroit and Los Angeles and Newark and cities all over the nation were drifting numbly to the brink, the guilt and fear that Dallas felt after Kennedy's murder propelled the oligarchy into a sort of ferocious attentiveness.

At that very moment in the city's history, the new white population, the T.I. types and the Yankees had developed a new white agenda around education and cultural issues — things like real art for the museum and a credible symphony — in which cause they were ready to enlist black support.

The North Dallas new folks would abandon the city's black community as soon as busing threatened real integration, but, at that crucial moment, they were there with outstretched arms. The black community found itself smothered between the panicky oligarchs on the one hand, who were afraid in their hearts that they had allowed the murder of the best white hope black people had ever known, and on the other hand the new "liberals," full of good causes and good advice, as long as the black people didn't try to put their own kind on the school board slate. In spite of this, the black community in Dallas has continued to change its own fate and the fate of the city.

In looking too closely at the black community, it's possible to fail to see the forest, to forget that this was a city, after all, in which even the most vital interests and passionate obsessions of the white majority could be silenced by a sufficient show of authority. All it took was Walter Cronkite, really, wagging his finger and warning them that they would go to jail, be outcasts, and never see the boy scouts on parade again if they made trouble, and the entire white community willingly heeded the warning. Dallas was an enlightened, far-sighted, creative, tough-minded, totalitarian state, and the white people who ran it were able to run it that way because the white people who lived in it liked it that way. In that sense, black people in Dallas have had a much tougher job than merely achieving the same degree of freedom the white folks had. In Dallas, black people had to fight for freedoms that some white people never knew existed.

The single most important change in the structure of Dallas, as a city and as a society, was the destruction of the old at-large system, and it was achieved by the black community. Since the introduction of single-member districts, the entire city — including the white community — has become vastly more politicized. It is an utterly different place today than it was a mere eight years ago, and in that context and that sense, far from lagging behind, the black community in Dallas has provided the larger community with vital leadership.

Elsie Faye Heggins sat at the dais that the white city council had built for itself and talked back to the mayor for a good year or so before the real miracle of miracles happened: white council members started talking back to him, too. In the early 1980s, when the real estate developers who had dominated the city from the 1940s tried to ram new freeways and roads through the older city, in order to service their raw land developments out north, it was white councilmembers like Lee Simpson from East Dallas who struck back hardest and most effectively. As the 1980s progressed and the developers came back into North Dallas to build hotels and office buildings where they had already built expensive single-family neighborhoods, it was the oligarchy's very own constituency who fought them. The wealthy white North Dallas Republicans who owned those homes refused to sit back idly and watch more traffic congestion ruin their neighborhoods.

The oligarchy had lost its own constituency. People began to stick up for themselves in Dallas; ordinary citizens became involved, put their hands on the machinery and felt how it moved; the city started to get pluralistic and interesting, almost like America; it became a much more attractive place to new kinds of people from other kinds of places than it had been before; and, in all of this, the black community had led the way. Perhaps nothing says as much about the mentality of the old power structure as its insistence now that representative democratic government cannot work, that it is incapable of generating "policy," that it is inherently divisive, corrupting and will lead to vagrancy. What all of this would mean, if we took it seriously, is that the United States is doomed. It is a mindset still so separated from the assumptions that drive the nation that we are reminded of it by the old Dallas Morning News editorials of the early 1960s accusing the President of something very like treason.

The city, in fact, is still very new at this democracy business and is still learning the ropes, but it is already doing pretty well. Dallas County Commissioner John Wiley Price thinks that, if the new politics is still one or two steps short of being able to come up with the broad kind of decision-making that George Schrader calls "policy," it's because people in Dallas haven't learned yet how to form coalitions.

"In Dallas, I don't think there are real coalitions," Price said. "There seems to be an overt agenda to sabotage coalitions."

Price is in his mid-thirties. When he was elected to the Dallas County Commissioner's Court in 1984, becoming one of four county leaders on the commission, he also became the most powerful black elected official in Dallas County since Reconstruction. He is typical of the kind of bright, tough new leadership that is bubbling up now out of the black community. Price came up fighting the black ministerial alliance and the old ways. He commands the respect of both the streetfighters from Fair Park homeowners days and the sophisticated Zan Holmes crowd. He moved to Dallas in 1970 at the age of 19. He grew up in nearby Forney — the town R. L. Thornton used as his metaphor for a place with no problems and no opportunity. He agreed with Thornton. He moved to Dallas "for the same reason everybody did," he says, "because there were jobs."

John Wiley Price had no personal experience with Dallas history in the 1960s when he got to town. His first political involvement was in the fight for community control of the Martin Luther King Community Center. Originally, it had been the idea of the white community, including many of the white liberals left over from the T.I. days, that the black community center in South Dallas should be governed by a board selected from the entire city, so that it would not be under narrow, parochial (black) domination, giving it more a sense of Dallas as a whole. That idea failed, and John Price was one of the passionate young volunteers who pitched in with more seasoned people like Mrs. Heggins to see that it failed.

After the 1980 census, Price, who was by then administrative assistant to Cleophas R. Steele, a black judge, helped lead a reapportionment campaign aimed at creating new black legislative districts at all levels of government. White liberals including State Senator Oscar Mauzy and Congressman Martin Frost fought against the new black districts, which would have threatened their own positions. They succeeded in defeating the creation of a minority congressional seat for Dallas, saving Frost's post for then but leaving a very bitter taste in the mouths of many of the new black political leaders.

One post that Price and his allies did succeed in getting redrawn was the county commission seat that includes most of the county's black population. In an intense battle for that seat in 1984, Price defeated his old ally, Mrs. Heggins. Now Price finds himself at the head of a very complex black community, dealing with what is sometimes a politically and morally unevolved white community. His view of the path ahead is more political than Cottrell's business strategy, but the core of it is the same — independence first, then coalition.

"Black people in Dallas need to acquire capital instead of jobs. They need to recognize that you don't own a job, a job owns you. But the route to doing that is through achieving true, full enfranchisement in the political arena and financial independence in the business arena."

From a position of unfettered power, power for which they owe white people nothing, Price believes black people in Dallas will one day reach back into the white community to achieve true coalition, rather than accommodation and dependency.

The problem faced by the black community, or any other subcommunity seeking coalitions in Dallas for that matter, is that the iron grip of the oligarchy has been so recently broken and the experience of American democratic pluralistic politics is so new, that there is no developed system of coalition to join.

"People have got to learn how to reach out and form coalitions around issues," Price says. "That just doesn't happen yet in Dallas, and it has to happen. People have to learn how to identify areas of mutual interest and coalesce around them, before we can move ahead and begin to solve a lot of the major problems before us." When coalitions begin to form, they will generate consensus — the political building material of public policy.

In this sense, John Wiley Price and other thinkers like him in the black community are pulling the larger community forward with them. They are forcing their way back into the domain from which all people in Dallas had been barred for so long by the oligarchy. In the battle for full enfranchisement and for truly representative government, the black community is going back in and reimposing the rule of law where for so long the only rule was authority, enforced by violence at one hand and accommodation at the other. The city, so long without real political legitimacy or direction, is being given the foundation of ideas it has so sorely lacked for so long.

There are still parts of Dallas that are awfully white, so white that a visitor from Detroit or Atlanta might feel he had stepped through time into a Perry Mason rerun, where black actors only show up once in a great while and one at a time, usually in the role of domestics or jazz musicians wearing berets. At the Galleria, an enormous and glittering new shopping mall in North Dallas, white people swirl from shop to shop on the weekends and whirl around on a large indoor ice-skating rink, at home with each other and at ease, as if finally the answer to it all really is that white people just want to have fun with other white people.

By the same token, there are parts of Dallas, in South Dallas on the other side of the Trinity River, where life and days and the business of getting along in the world are entirely black, where one can live almost without reference to white people.

Between the two extreme camps, there are a number of very civilized middle grounds, in the charming old deep-shaded neighborhoods of East Dallas, on the bluffs of Oak Cliff, and in the vast new housing tracts on the periphery where everybody is somebody from somewhere else anyway, where white and black people live in each

190

other's midst with very little friction.

If anything, a white newcomer from one of the busing enclaves in the suburban rings around cities of the North would be struck first by the absence in Dallas of the kind of dirty-mouthed, festered, aggressive racism that marks many of the northern white cities, especially where rioting occurred. Dallas didn't suffer those wounds and doesn't bear those scars. In that, there is promise. By evading the scarring of violence and the deep-harbored enmity violence breeds, maybe Dallas made of itself a place that will be able to reach solutions politically and without war.

The other thing a watchful newcomer must notice is an enormous social gulf between blacks and whites in Dallas in spite of it all — not that there isn't distance elsewhere, but in Dallas the distance spans a vast, formal, and unexplored reserve. The question is whether Dallas will find a peaceful political way to accomplish all of the painful communication other cities accomplished only in violence and whether it will accomplish that soon enough. There is all of the rage Zan Holmes talked about that didn't get out. There is all of the psychological self-mutilation white slave culture inflicted on itself that still has to be cured. There is all of the wonderful promise implicit in not having suffered certain wounds. The city hovers just above the peaks of enormous possibilities, some wonderful, some awful.

INDEX

INDEX